The God W̶

- and -

You Will Receive Power

by

Ian Petit OSB

New Life Publishing, Luton, UK

This edition published in 2004 by
New Life Publishing
15 Barking Close
Luton, LU4 9HG, UK

The God Who Speaks first published in 1989
by Darton Longman & Todd and reprinted in 1991 and 1992
You Will Receive Power first published in 1994
by Darton Longman & Todd and reprinted in 1998

ISBN 1 903623 17 0

Unless otherwise stated the biblical references in this
book are taken from *The Jerusalem Bible*, published and
copyright 1966, 1967 and 1968 by Darton, Longman
& Todd Ltd and Doubleday & Co. Inc.

The publishers would like to thank McCrimmon Publishing Co.
Ltd., for permission to quote from the author's contribution to
Anointed with the Spirit 1978 in the introduction to *The God Who Speaks*

British library Cataloguing in Publication Data.
A catalogue record for this book is available
from the British Library

Cover design by Yvonne Bell, www.vestments.co.uk.
Yvonne creates stoles, chasubles and copes
to individual design, often on silk.

New Life Publishing, Luton UK

Contents

The God Who Speaks

You Will Receive Power

Further copies of Fr. Ian's books

God is Not Angry and **Your Sins are Forgiven**
The God Who Speaks and **You Will Receive Power**
This is My Body and **How Can I Pray ?**

*are available by mail order
from*

Goodnews Books & Audio

Tel: 01582 571011
Fax: 01582 571012
email: orders@goodnewsbooks.net
www.goodnewsbooks.net

Send for a Catalogue of Christian Books

Preface

I wonder if we are right in imagining that every Christian has been evangelised? The gospel message is far-ranging, and it is possible to get attached to our own part of it and miss the central point. So much depends on how we were introduced to it. From my experience of counselling, I have discovered that many of us have built our religion on secondary truths, and although the central truth has never been denied, it has never become a living force in our lives.

I see this as a serious sickness in the Church, because if Christianity is not experienced as life-giving, then either we heroically embrace something which is not the gospel or we abandon religion. You cannot put your faith in what you do not know, and when there is no faith in what God has done through the death and rising of his Son, then can we honestly say there is new life?

In this book I want to spell out in very simple language the central truth of the gospel. The trouble with stating profound truths simply is that it leaves much unsaid, so misunderstandings can arise. But then accuracy can also have its problems, because in the desire to be exact subclause gets added to subclause, and clarity is sacrificed in the quest for precision.

I, who had the advantage of studying some theology, managed to miss the central point of the gospel, so what of those who have not had that advantage? I do not blame my teachers, but I do blame that image I had of God long before I opened any theology book. That is why I want to go back to basics and spell out the foundations.

I write for those who honestly recognise their difficulty in understanding and living out the gospel, and for those who plod along with only a very hazy comprehension. I also write for those who have set out on the Christian way but become disenchanted and given up, and for others who are not from a Christian background and who may know little about the gospel.

We are all pilgrims, we are all on a journey. Most of this book is my travelogue. I offer it in the hope that it might help others on their journey.

IAN PETIT OSB

Introduction

I have to confess that I only really began to understand the central truths of the gospel after I had been a priest for many years. The crucial time of enlightenment for me came at the end of the 1960s and in the early 1970s.

I had been one of a team of four monks who had been sent out in 1956 from Ampleforth Abbey in Yorkshire to St Louis, Missouri, USA. Our task was to found a monastery and a school. The years there had been very demanding and from about 1967 onwards I was at a very low ebb both physically and spiritually. Weariness and overwork can bring about a spiritual crisis. I was heading for some of the roughest years of my life. It was not just dryness; I was on the verge of complete disillusionment. I had given my all, left home and country, worked till fit to drop; and here I was empty, tired, and even questioning the principles I had held as gospel truth. I cannot pretend that the insights brought about by Vatican II helped me much; they only confirmed in me that there was something very

1

amiss in the way I had picked up religion and monasticism.

Quite close to our Priory, there was a Visitation convent. I was one of their confessors and I often gave them spiritual conferences. In August 1968, just after I had come back from my summer holidays, they phoned me to say they had had some exciting talks on prayer given by the Dominican, Fr Francis MacNutt, and a Baptist minister. When I went down to see them, I confess I could not understand what they were talking about. I heard about the Holy Spirit, the gift of tongues, the gifts of the Spirit, the Good News of the gospel. I did not know what all the excitement was about – it certainly was not my present experience, and I was highly suspicious of all this enthusiasm. Surely religion was meant to be much pain and struggle?

For a year I attended their prayer meetings. I had a love-hate relationship with all I saw going on. I certainly needed help, and I wanted all this love, joy and peace, but there was much that turned me off. Fortunately, I saw that my hesitancy was due to cultural rather than theological reasons. But I have to admit I was very suspicious of these Protestant people.

In August 1969, health intervened, I lost weight rapidly, exhaustion was diagnosed and that October I was packed off home to Europe for the rest of the year. I did not want to go – being busy can stop you from thinking a thing through; now I would have time, and I might

2

think myself not only out of the priesthood, but even out of Christianity.

I rapidly recovered my physical health, though sleep was a problem. I travelled much, rested, walked, but spiritually I seemed to have died. I could not pray, and I seemed quite incapable of communicating my desolation to anyone. It is virtually impossible to explain what a priest in crisis feels like; after all, you are meant to be an expert in spiritual matters, so people do not expect you ever to have a crisis in that realm.

At the end of the year, it was suggested I should stay longer, but I felt I could not spend my life resting. It was decided that I should return to St Louis, although I was not to take up my teaching yet.

On my return, of course, I went down to the Visitation convent. There they were, all praising God; and the fascination rose up in me again. How those sisters had grown! It was then that I heard about Pecos – a Benedictine Priory that had gone charismatic. Benedictines would be safe; so off I went down there.

I talked with Fr David Geraets, who has since become their abbot, and I told him I had read everything I could lay my hands on, I had attended many prayer meetings, but I could not experience any of this peace they all talked about. I had even begun to wonder if I was damned or possessed. He alarmed me by asking me if I had ever spoken in tongues. I told him that I had a real problem with 'tongues' – why should an intelligent God want an intelligent creature to pray to him in an unintelligible way? He explained that it was sometimes necessary to do something we could not understand, because with priests and ministers we run the danger of having only intellectual faith. We know answers; and we think we believe because we can give an answer. He suggested that launching out into tongues would be a real act of faith for me. So I explained, with much embarrassment, that as a small boy I had often pretended that I was a foreigner and I would jabber on the buses in London with my brothers and sisters. I have a good ear and I can imitate French, Spanish and Italian sounds, even Oriental noises! I must confess I thought that that would floor him. But not at all! 'Oh, you are lucky,' he replied. 'You've got the mechanics. All you have to do, is to submit that to God.' I could not accept that.

That afternoon I went for a walk in the mountains surrounding the Priory. It was a windy day and the clouds were fast moving and low. I can remember standing there in the hills shaking my fist at heaven. 'Why don't you speak? Do you have to drive a man mad before you will answer?' I was angry; but nothing happened – no parting of the clouds, no light. That night after compline, several people staying at the Priory asked to be prayed over. I had seen this happen many times, I had often

4

stood in the circle and had even prayed aloud. This time as we were praying, I heard one monk praying in tongues quite softly. I felt, 'I might as well try this out. I'll go to the end of this branch to see if anything is there'. So, in cold deliberation I committed my voice to God and did my party-piece. Nothing happened. The people we prayed for looked more dead than any people we had prayed for before; but more important to me, nothing happened in me. So that was the end; I was grateful none of my own brethren had been present to see me make a fool of myself.

Next morning I awoke feeling very foolish. While waiting for morning office to begin, I pulled out my New Testament and opened it at random. My eyes fell on the text: 'Go, I am sending you far away to the Gentiles.' I do not think I really understood the text, but it was as though I heard someone say those words right down inside me as I read them. You must understand that after almost two years of nearly total silence, this was a profound moment. I remember closing the book in a hurry and saying, 'That is for St Paul. Not me'. But something had happened.

That day I listened to talks being given to the retreatants, and the message was very simple and clear. 'I want men of faith in my Church. I do not want men who know everything. I want men who will believe in me, who will do what I say. Even walk on water if I should command them.' Did all this happen because of this 'talking in tongues'? Was it really 'talking in tongues'? I do not know the answers to these questions; all I know is something changed. I felt compelled to go on exploring.

A few months later, I was at Ann Arbor. I met there a Fr George Kosicki CSB. He told me that he was starting a small house of prayer for priests, where we could honestly ask all the questions we wanted, where we could search together into this renewal. I told him I was his first candidate. So having gone up to Ann Arbor for a weekend, I actually stayed up in the Detroit area for nearly five months. The experience was not easy. I was living with a group of people who expected things to happen. Things did happen but I was suspicious that we read more into the happenings than was there. I feared the text in Scripture referring to those who did great things in the name of Christ but in the end even Jesus claimed not to know them. But one thing made me stay – I have never experienced such love. I had every argument against them and what they honestly stood for, but they never grew impatient with me and were very loving. This must be of God.

After three months or more I had to confess to Fr George that really inside me I was still lost. I had learnt much, I could pray aloud, I could raise my arms without too much embarrassment, I even sang in tongues when the group praised in that way – but I could not honestly say with conviction 'Alleluia'. George asked me if I was still using the gift of tongues. I told him that I joined in the singing when the group did. But he said, 'No, you should use it in your own personal, private prayer. You had an experience with the gift, you must now consciously use it.' So I began for a few minutes each day doing what he told me. On the third day, when I had just finished doing this, and I was turning round to come back to the house, I suddenly understood the gospel: 'Why are you so full of fear? Why are you always trying to win my favour? Can you not see I have sent you my Son and he has reconciled you. I want you to live in him and live as son.' I did not hear these words, it was as though I spoke them to myself within myself. But now I had come to understand. I was through the wall; I saw the Good News, understood at last what it meant to be in Christ Jesus.

Looking back on those years of personal trauma, I can now see a meaning in them, although at the time it was not at all clear what was happening and I imagined that I was on my way out of the priesthood and even of the Church. I am amazed to think, after all my theological and scriptural training, that I had such a wrong understanding of the gospel. I know now that God had to deal with this misunderstanding but I fought tooth and nail against his reordering of my thoughts, fearing that I was being tempted to doubt and abandon the

7

very foundation on which my spiritual life had
been built. I now see that that very foundation
had to be destroyed. It was not that my theological training was wrong; what was wrong was
the base on which it rested. God, for me, was
someone to fear, someone I had to placate,
humour, and I shaped everything I learnt to fit
in with this misconception. God had to break
the stranglehold my wrong picture of him had
over me, but as he did this, I imagined that my
faith was being shattered, when all the time he
was shattering the bogey that I thought was
God.

I have written this book to share something
of the fruit of that crisis in my life. My new
understanding did not come in flashing revelations – indeed it has been a long and often
painful journey into light. But I thank God for
it now, as I am able to comprehend how the
gospel can appear anything but life-giving for
some people. I understand how people can
listen to the gospel and not see it as the
solution. My life was not wicked, nor peppered
with great sins, but it was full of *my* directing,
my efforts, *my* making myself holy. I needed
to learn that that sort of life has been dealt with
by Christ's dying and rising. That is what this
book is about. It is not a testimony, though I
do share much of my own experience; nor is
it a book about the charismatic renewal, and
speaking in tongues. Rather I am trying to show
how basic misconceptions can persist in spite of

sound teaching. So, as you read, be honest with yourself and admit your basic feelings and ideas about God. These may have to surface into the light, but as we confess our wrong ideas and attitudes, the Spirit of God brings about the forgiveness and healing that Jesus won for us at such great cost.

1

Beyond Ourselves

Since the Spirit is our life, let us be directed by the Spirit. (Gal. 5:26)

I cannot remember my first thoughts of God or when I was first told about him. I came from a Catholic family, so very early on I would have heard about God, and I would have been taken to church at a young age. Somewhere along the line, I picked up the idea that God was not someone I was too keen to know. I heard that he knew everything, and I found that disconcerting for it meant I had no secrets from him. I was told he was good, and that was uncomfortable because I was *not* good; it was not that I was wicked, but I certainly was not good. How deep first impressions must go for surely I must have heard that God loved me, but that did not seem to erase my conviction that he was someone to fear. I do not know who communicated that fear to me – I am sure no one taught it directly. I must have picked up many different impressions and built them into a picture. From my own experience of trying to teach others about God, I realise how very difficult it is to communicate the truth; it is so easy to make God too hard or too soft, but how very important those early communications are.

From these first, rather negative impressions other ideas grew. The stories from the Old Testament did not improve the picture, but rather confirmed the notion that this God was not to be meddled with. I found church services boring, as I suppose most children do, and slowly, without actually saying it in so many words, I concluded that God was a bit of a spoil-sport frowning on anything that was enjoyable and promoting anything that hurt or was dull.

I would not say I was an irreligious child. Put me under a beech tree just after its leaves had come out, show me a sunset or a magnificent view and my spirit would soar. I could stay for hours just staring at the beauty of nature – a clear sky washed clean by the rain, a wild seascape, an autumn wood. I do not think it was just sensuous; deep down I felt I was in contact with something, or someone, sacred. I found poetry had the same effect on me, and when I heard about the great god Pan I half wondered if I had met him in the woods; and I grew fearful in case this is what the Gospels meant when they talked about 'loving the world'. All this set up a strange tension in me, for I could see no connection between what I

11

was finding in the fields and what I learnt about in church. In fact, it has taken most of my life to bring these two together, and the marriage is still fairly fragile – first impressions do die hard.

I believe it was my spirit that was being touched at those moments when I seemed to be drawn out of myself and in touch with something 'other'. It is strange that my religion which should have been all about the spirit never touched me in that way but just brought fear and dread. Later the sense of mystery did appear but it was always mixed with anxiety. We all have a spirit and it would be good if you could try to see how your spirit may have made itself known to you. Most of us experience sudden questions that rise up from apparently nowhere: 'What is it all for? Where am I going?' These questions are uncomfortable and we can dismiss them and fail to respond to a moment of grace. There are other times when we seem to be taken out of ourselves, as though we were lifted up above our life and see things from a different perspective. It may be when walking in nature, or listening to music, or reading poetry; for each of us it will be different. We cannot make this sort of thing happen; they are moments of grace and we should learn to welcome these ambassadors from the land deep within ourselves. Too often we let our false pictures of God inhibit us and we ignore the promptings of our spirit. Or perhaps we are suspicious of such promptings because we are afraid our friends might laugh at us if we share them. We find it so difficult to trust our own experience of God and frequently listen to the voice of authority or of others rather than listen to what God is saying to us through our spirit.

Body, soul and spirit

We are more than just body and soul; we are body, soul and *spirit*. For years I thought my soul *was* my spirit, and it was only after someone had pointed out to me the passage in Hebrews where it says that the word of God 'can slip through the place where the soul is divided from the spirit' (4:12) that I began to be aware of this separation of soul and spirit. Every time I met the word 'spirit' in Scripture I paid special attention and I began to see that there was a whole way of knowing that did not involve the reasoning process. With my mind, I can come to conclusions through a process of deductive thinking and I can explain afterwards just how I reached those conclusions. But when I know something in my spirit, I cannot say how I know; all I know is, I know.

Our thought process is very complex. Truths are conveyed to us through ideas and reasoning. But these are limited and cannot fully contain or convey the reality they wish to express. There is a reality that lies beyond words and cannot be reached by words, thoughts or ideas.

13

I understand revelation to be when God imparts a truth without me having to go through a process of deduction. I cannot make this happen, but I can allow stillness to be part of my life, so that when the small voice of God speaks, in my stillness I will be able to hear it.

I think at this point I should attempt a brief definition of body, soul and spirit. I do so hesitantly as I realise how difficult it is to describe adequately the make-up of a human being, but some sort of definition is needed. Through the body we are 'physical' beings and partake in the material world. Through the soul we are 'rational' beings, able to live in the immaterial as well as the material world and bringing into play our reason, our will, our imagination and our emotions. Through the spirit we are 'spiritual' beings and operate in a realm beyond the reach of body and soul. It is through our spirit that God communicates with us and that we receive the gift of the Holy Spirit; intuition and inspiration are important here.

It might be helpful to use the word 'heart' in place of spirit, but I am a little reluctant to do so as the word 'heart' is often identified with feeling, emotion, sentiment as when someone says, 'he touched my heart'. There is another sense for the word 'heart' as when we say, 'my heart is not in it' or 'in my heart I feel that is wrong': here my inmost being is in question and that is what I want to call my spirit. The best example I know which shows someone coming to knowledge through the spirit is Peter's declaration that Jesus is the Christ, the Son of the living God; look at Jesus' response to Peter: 'Blessed are you, Simon son of Jonah, you are a happy man! Because it was not flesh and blood that revealed this to you but my Father in heaven' (Matt. 16:17). Peter had not come to this truth through any rational process ('flesh and blood') but because the Father had revealed it to him.

In the western world much effort has been spent on developing our bodies and souls, but because of the vague ideas we have about spirit, we have not developed that side of ourselves to the same extent. We are suspicious of inspiration – we are factual, practical and logical people. But since God communicates himself to us through our spirit, how important it is that we develop our spiritual side. The need to learn about the realm of the spirit is all the more pressing because of the growing interest in the occult and the current fascination with Eastern mysticism; many people, disenchanted with materialism, are turning to the world of the spirit, and it is essential for Christians to be familiar with this world. This does not mean that we are to ignore our body and soul; these are to be developed as well although not to the neglect of our spirit. We will look at how we can nurture our spirit in more detail later. First of all let us look at things with which we are more familiar: our body and soul. As we do this, we must avoid putting ourselves into compartments; we are one person who can operate in three different spheres.

Through our body we are privileged to be part of the material world. Some people imagine that to be spiritual entails rising above the body and escaping into a rarefied atmosphere of the spirit. God made the world of matter and he saw and declared it was good; so it must not be spurned. Think what it means to be able to touch and feel, to put things together and take them apart. What a wonderful thing colour is – how dull it would be to see everything as a black and white photograph. Angels cannot see, touch, hear or smell. They have no contact with the material world as we do. God's plan was that we should be part of this material universe, so he fashioned us from the very dust of the earth.

Try to think of some of the things you particularly like doing; it may be playing a sport, walking in the countryside, cooking a meal, doing embroidery – all such things are to be enjoyed and we should not despise them. I can remember the first time I learnt to water-ski. I am a sun lover, and when I was sent to be part of a monastic foundation in the United States, it was an extraordinary experience to see so much blue sky and to find the sun was actually too hot. I learnt to water-ski in Michigan. It all happened on one of those glorious summer days that one thought only

16

existed in holiday brochures. Everything was sparkling, the lake was warm and the sky was a sharp, deep blue. Being something of an athlete and having had experience on roller and ice-skates, to everyone's amazement, I managed to get up on the skis straightaway. What a sensation it was to fizz across the top of that blue lake with cool spray splashing all over my body. One might say that it was all very sensuous, but in some way I felt that I had touched God, or, more amazingly, that he had touched me. It is hard to describe what a profound effect that experience had on me; having felt God's touch there, I began to see his touch was always present, hidden in less spectacular moments. Thus through bodily pleasures God is able to speak to our spirit, and, as I said earlier, we should be careful not to put ourselves into compartments and to separate rigidly our experiences into those of the body, those of the soul and those of the spirit.

When Genesis tells us that God created the human race, there seems to be a change in his way of creating. Instead of just saying, 'Let there be man', he says: 'Let us make man in our own image, in the likeness of ourselves and let them be masters of the fish of the sea, the birds of heaven, the cattle, all the wild beasts and all the reptiles that crawl upon the earth' (1:26). It seems as though there was a committee meeting in the Godhead over the creation of this all-important creature. We were to be masters over the world of matter and in order for this to happen we needed to be more than body: we needed an intelligence.

So we are not just to be *part* of the material world; we are to be *masters* of it, and for this we need to be able to know it and understand it – we need to bring our soul into operation. What an extraordinary thing it is to know something; not just to see it, but to know and recognise it for what it is. Through our observance of the world around us, we have been able to see that things do not just happen, and we have discovered that matter is subject to laws. We are not always able to trace exactly why certain things happen; all we can say is they have a nature which makes them act or react in a certain way. When God made the world he did not make it complete and fully developed. He planned to have his world explored and developed by the creatures he chose to be its masters. What ingenious creatures we are; just a simple glance at what we have achieved is indeed staggering. We have learnt to fly, and that at great speed; we can talk to people on the other side of the world, and we can even see what they are doing at the moment they do it; we have put men on the moon and brought them back again.

Not only are we able to draw knowledge and insights from the material world around us, but we can also enter the immaterial world of abstract ideas. Our thinking is not confined to what we can imagine; we can also deal with abstract ideas – we can juggle with concepts and draw conclusions after complex processes of deduction. So our thinking is not limited to the material world; we can explore the world of ideas. We are like unto God in that we are reasoning beings. In giving us a soul, God gave us power to reason, to remember, to experience emotion and to decide on a course of action. We were not called to be robots doing the will of God automatically. God gave us the incredible privilege of being responsible creatures. Free will is not the liberty to do what we want; it is the liberty to do willingly what we were created for.

As with our body, I think it would be good if you could consider the ways in which you take pleasure in the gifts of the soul; for example some of us are very imaginative and enjoy the riches our imaginations can offer; others of us take satisfaction in solving problems and thinking things through logically; and still others are able to grapple with complex, abstract ideas. At school I never seemed to shine at my studies – my gifts were athletic. So when I began to teach I felt very much at one with students who said they did not understand the lessons. I knew the misery of not knowing what masters were talking about, and dreading that this would be exposed by my being asked a question. School life did have its special agonies, and so I became very

19

inventive in trying to show slow students that
they could cope with these intellectual gymnas-
tics. It was a long process but what joy there
was when one day their eyes lit up and they
said: 'Now I see; now I've got it.' Twenty years
further on, it is marvellous to meet some of
these 'slow' students and to see what fine,
competent and capable young men they have
grown into.

Even though our soul can deal with abstract
ideas and the immaterial, it is unable to reach
the world of spirit. We can grapple with spiritual concepts and speculate about them, but the
world of spirit is beyond our soul. Hence God
also made us spirit so that he could communicate his will to us, and have us ponder that
communication and work out how to put it into
action, and finally call our whole being into
operation. The human being is God's prize
creation. We are not just pure animal, nor just
pure intelligence, nor just pure spirit. We
partake in all three worlds and we are called to
a harmonious unity of spirit, soul and body –
in that order. We are not to lose our earthiness,
nor our brilliance, nor the power to walk in the
cool of the evening with the One who made us.

It is fairly obvious when we are operating in
our body. When we see, touch or hear things,
we use our body. It is interesting to note that
we do not say 'My eyes see' or 'My nose smells',
but 'I see', 'I smell' – we identify ourselves
with our body. When we operate in our soul,

20

understanding how we act is not such a simple matter. Clearly, I can decide to think about someone, but actually what I do to make that happen is not very easy to describe. You, surely, have had the experience of trying to remember something which seems just out of reach of your mind. We often say: 'It is on the tip of my tongue.' Try describing what you do when you try to remember; it is difficult to explain how you do it. It is not like looking for the car keys because then you can turn out pockets, search under the cushions of chairs and sort through your desk; but when trying to remember something we do not use any muscles or perform any obvious actions. Yet, we are able to remember. We can understand what it means to think, act, call to mind, have an emotion, but the actual process involved in making these things happen is a very baffling one. So, trying to describe how our soul actually works is difficult. Because our spirit has been rather neglected, it is even harder to explain what happens when our spirit operates. I suppose most of us have experienced intuition. Somehow we *know* something without being aware of how or even why. It can be a very strong and certain knowledge, and when we discover that it turns out to be true, we say, 'I just knew I was right'. It is an area we are suspicious about, and of course we can be mistaken because not everything in the spiritual world is good and holy; there are evil

21

spirits. Jesus promised to send his Holy Spirit of truth to us. While he was on earth he taught the truth and before he left he promised to send his followers the Spirit of truth to be their continual guide. Spirit speaks to spirit, and it is in our spirit that the Holy Spirit communicates God's word. How necessary it is for us to understand more about our own spirit, but first of all we need to know how our spirit lost its ascendency over our body and soul.

2

Like God but Not God

You have made him a little less than a god.
(Ps. 8:5)

We were made to be *like* God, but not to *be* God – this is the drama behind the story of the Fall, and it has ever since remained the drama for all human life. God endowed human beings with extraordinary gifts and powers; he made them in his own image and likeness, and placed them in authority over the beautiful world he had created. Alas, they abused their privileged position, and in rejecting their creaturehood they made a bid to rival God. The story of the Fall isn't just about how God's special creatures went wrong; it is about how those special creatures and all their descendants became damaged and bent, while remaining exceedingly gifted.

When science looks at creation, it does so from a scientific point of view. It asks the questions: what? how? and when? The Bible approaches creation in a different way: it asks who? and why? There should be no disharmony between these two disciplines provided each keeps to its own field. Once religion tries to answer scientific questions, then trouble occurs, and the same is true when science enters the realm of religion. So when we read Scripture we must not approach it with a scientific mind. We need to know that the words used often have deep symbolic meanings, and we should avoid getting hung up on words, for, after all, it is the events, not the words, that are important; so we need to search deeply for the inner meaning. That is why we must pray to the Holy Spirit of God and ask him to enlighten our spirits, so that our minds can be flooded with truth. I used to read Scripture trying like mad to understand it, hoping that then I would come to believe it. I now see that I had things upside down – I ought first to believe Scripture and then work like mad to understand it.

I never got very much from the story of creation in Genesis until a friend began to unwrap it for me. I was amazed at how much could be uncovered once I moved beyond the plain meaning of the words. I began to see how much my mind had been influenced by western pragmatic thinking, and I needed to be taught how to think in a new way. Could this be why fairy stories have such an appeal for us? Is there a part of us which is undeveloped and starved? When you see the sheer goodness of God, then the enormity of the sin that said, 'I do not need you; I'll go my own way', becomes shockingly apparent.

We cannot all become scholars in Scripture, but we need to find some wise guide to lead us to see beyond the simple story that the words tell. When I first began reading Genesis I found many questions arose in my mind and I would go to books to seek clarification, but I would often be discouraged because I did not understand what they were driving at. Now, quite simply, I pray and tell God that I do not understand his word and I ask for the Spirit's help. This does not mean that I get instant illuminations; often several weeks will go by, but during that time I am taking steps to find answers. I ask friends, I look in different commentaries, and because my mind is pondering the question, that means I am on the lookout and as soon as some insight on the matter appears, I am quick to notice it. Slowly answers do emerge. At first it was rather a painstaking process, but gradually I have acquired knowledge and I have built up a store of information. It is like doing a jigsaw – initially nothing seems to connect, then you get little islands of two or three pieces; these then fit together excitingly and suddenly the picture emerges.

In the first chapters of Genesis, God is telling us about the beginnings. Obviously there was no scribe witnessing the events. God inspired the author to say what he did say. The scope of this chapter is not to try and decide who wrote the account, nor to understand how he or she was inspired. I want to look at the text and dig out its deeper meanings.

We are clearly told that everything God did was good, and yet, deep down, we all have a tendency to blame God when things go wrong. It is interesting how insurance companies refer to 'acts of God' when they are dealing with natural disasters. Genesis is stating clearly that God does not do evil. It is true that it does not explain where evil comes from, but I think we ought to resist the easy way out of blaming God for what goes wrong.

The origin of evil is a question that taxes us all. I knew someone who had a very mischievous daughter. Long before she reached the so-called age of reason, she was into every form of trouble. No one taught her to be naughty; she just seemed to know by instinct what was forbidden. I used to say jokingly that she was proof of original sin; where there was trouble she was in the midst of it. More seriously, we who have passed the age of reason, can detect in ourselves the same trait. Something is wrong with us all. How this should be so, if God made us good in the first place, is something that has bothered mankind since the whole thing began. I do not know where evil comes from, but I know it exists and I can detect it in myself. From the book of Genesis I learn there was a tempter, but where he, or she, came from I do not know. In the book of

Revelation (12:7) we read that there was a battle in heaven. We have no details; we are not told what the battle was about. All we know is that Satan and his followers were cast out of heaven. So even before the creation of the material universe, God had an enemy, and this enemy was bent on spoiling God's new creation. How Satan actually came to do wrong, we do not know, but if God is good, are we right to blame him for the evil we find here on earth?

We should also note that there are two accounts of creation given. This could help us from getting hung up on taking the seven day account literally. In the first account there seems to be a gradation from material things to living plants to animals and finally to the human race, while in the second account people come on the scene fairly early. In the first account we are told that human beings were made in the image and likeness of God, but from the second account we learn that they are unlike God because they are made from the same stuff as the animals. Yet, although they may come from the soil of the earth with the animals, it is clear that they are different from the animals, for God gave the creatures 'all the foliage of plants for food' (1:30) whereas man and woman were given a garden, a park, an attractive place, and it was called 'Delight' (Eden) indicating that they could appreciate beauty. God settled the

27

human beings in this garden and commanded
them to cultivate and take care of it.

We are told about the trees in the garden
and how Adam is invited to eat of them, and
by this we understand that he is invited to
explore the richness of the world that he has
been asked to master. Two trees in particular
are mentioned; one is the tree of life and the
other is the tree of knowledge of good and evil.
The tree of life stands for God, and the human
family are invited to draw their life from him
recognising their dependence on him. With
regard to the tree of knowledge of good and
evil, God expressly forbids Adam from even
touching it. It is interesting to notice that Satan
questioned Eve about this command and not
Adam; Eve had not received the command
directly from God and second-hand commands
are less forceful than first. What are we to learn
from this prohibition? Namely that it is God's
prerogative to know good and evil; it is his right
to decide what is good and what is evil. In
Scripture the word 'know' has the sense of personal experience, and in forbidding man and
woman to eat of this tree God is, as it were,
saying: 'I do not want you to experience evil.
Leave it to me to make decisions with regard
to what is good and what is not good for you.
Trust in me and obey me.' Here God is treating
Adam as *someone*, someone responsible for
himself. Human beings are not robots; we are
invited to be stewards of God's earth; we will

28

make many decisions as stewards, but we are
not lords of the earth and therefore must not
make decisions regarding what is good and what
is evil. That is the prerogative of God alone.
We have been made like God, but we are not
God. Love is based on choice. It is not love if
it is not chosen. What an extraordinary compli-
ment God pays to the human race in that he
makes this creature like unto himself and then
invites each individual to say freely: 'I choose
you as my God, my source of life.'

In the last chapter I pointed out that we are
not just body and soul, but we are body, soul
and spirit. This truth made a tremendous difference for me in my understanding of the story
of the Fall. For if God communicates with us
through our spirit, then anything that can
prevent God from doing this will have a devastating effect on us. See how the tempter invites
Eve to meet the needs of her body and soul,
but not of her spirit. 'The woman saw that the
tree was good to eat and pleasing to the eye';
she also saw that 'it was desirable for the knowledge it could give' (3:6). No directing came
through her spirit, where God communicates.
God, whom Adam and Eve had experienced as
utterly trustworthy, is now made to appear by
Satan as not totally dependable, and the
tragedy is that they trusted the one they did
not know, and doubted God whom they had
experienced as good. Satan achieved his end –
he made Adam and Eve forsake God's way of

guidance, and rely for enlightenment on their body and soul. In doing this the human spirit became darkened and we lost the indwelling, guiding Spirit of God. While human beings still remain extraordinarily gifted creatures, we no longer have the inner illumination, and our centre, instead of being God, has shifted to ourselves. We have replaced the light that came from the all-wise God with the light that comes from our own mind, which is incapable of knowing God himself, and can only speculate about him.

How does this affect us?

But what do these remote events say to us who live at such an immense distance from them? If we look honestly into ourselves, I think we will find that we are very much sons and daughters of Adam and Eve. They doubted God's word; have we ever detected the same trait in ourselves? Do we ever find our minds judging God's word? Do not misunderstand me; we must use our minds to comprehend God's word, but when this is hard to do, we can be tempted to judge it or even doubt it. For example, we read in Romans 6 that we are dead to sin. My reaction to that has been to think to myself: 'Not yet; would that I were dead to it.' There my mind is judging Scripture to be wrong and my understanding to be right. It is not a very surprising mistake to make in this instance because, alas, all of us experience that we do commit sins, and if that is so, then how can we be dead to sin? The reason we continue to sin is because we do not stand on the truth that with Christ we have died to the Adam way of life and that there is available to us now the power of the Risen Christ. It is not enough to know this in theory; in some way our belief has to be so real that we can take hold of that truth and actually experience its validity. We carry on sinning because our faith is very weak. We may *know* the truth but it is the acting out of the truth that is so difficult for us. The Holy Spirit can reach your spirit and teach you directly; I can only reach your mind, and that might start a whole deductive process which will only cloud the issue. I will return to this point in a later chapter.

Thus it is very easy for us to doubt God's word. The point I am making is a subtle one; I am not suggesting that we should be gullible, for God made us intelligent creatures, and in the parable of the sower Jesus tells us that when anyone hears the word 'without understanding' then the evil one can snatch it out of his heart (Matt. 13:19). We must allow our minds to be illumined by the word, for this is to live by the Spirit.

Sins of unbelief are not confined to unbelievers. If we want to know what we really believe, we should not ask ourselves 'What do I believe?' because it is all too easy to give lists

31

of things. If we want to know what we believe, we should look and see how we live our life. We might find that the bold words we utter when we profess our faith, are just words when we come down to the nitty-gritty of life. For example, I have found myself, on coming home rather late from a prayer meeting and remembering that I had forgotten to say the Evening Prayer of the Church, wondering if I should then sit down and pray the Evening Prayer. One side of me said, 'You've been praying all evening, surely that was Evening Prayer', while the other part of me was all for fulfilling the letter of the law. That showed what my real attitude was towards God – I could profess with my mouth that he was Father, but in fact my relationship with him was one of anxiety and tension.

In the next chapters we will see how God has restored his indwelling Spirit to our spirit through the death and resurrection of Jesus Christ, but can we honestly say that we live by that Spirit when so many of our decisions are prompted by our body or soul? It is fairly easy to see when it is our body that moves us into action. I am sure you have experienced making resolutions and found that you did not keep them. Maybe you decided that you were eating too many delicacies, say for example cream cakes or rich desserts, and you felt the resolution was firm and serious; but when the cake or dessert was presented, it was just too tempting to resist. There always seems some good reason to say 'just this time'.

Our soul can put us into action in a variety of ways. When I decide to do something because I like it, then my emotions are at work. Or I may decide not to do something because I do not like doing that sort of thing. Fear can prevent us from asking a question; we do not want to appear ignorant, so fear stops us doing the wise thing. When I do something because I want to, then it is my will that is the driving force behind my action. I may want to watch a certain television programme, so I make sure I get into the room first and put the television on before anyone else arrives. The most subtle and often the most deceptive way that the soul directs my actions is through my mind. I now decide to act or not to act according to whether I agree or do not agree. I do something because I hold it to be wise and right, or I refuse to do something because I think it to be wrong; for instance I could go round bathing all the babies in town because it seems like a good idea, but God may not actually want me to do that. Here it is my mind that becomes the final arbitrator and not God's word. All these three faculties – emotions, will and mind – belong to my soul. I think it might be helpful at this point for you to try and recognise the ways in which your soul prompts you to action; each of us is different and for some of us our mind will be the driving force in our lives, while for others our will or our emotions predominate. It is good to be aware of these tendencies and to have some understanding of the way we tick.

Jesus said that we must live by every word that comes out of the mouth of God (Matt. 4:4). It is in our spirit that God reveals his word to us and it is in our spirit that the full content of the word can be grasped. Our minds can appreciate the word but because they are not spirit they cannot take in the spiritual content without the aid of the Holy Spirit. 'What is born of the flesh is flesh; what is born of the Spirit is spirit' (John 3:6). In passing we need to note that the word 'flesh' here does not mean body; it refers to that way of life which does not live by the word of God but lives instead according to its own guidance. I will take this point up again in a later chapter when I will show how respectability can become a subtle substitute for Christianity.

When Adam and Eve chose to live independently of God, they cut themselves off from the guiding light of the Holy Spirit. The children born from Adam and Eve are still gifted children; they have bodies by which they can touch, use and appreciate the world of matter; they have souls that enable them to remember, to think, to decide and to experience emotion; but they lack God's light in their spirits, and since self has replaced God as centre, all these wonderful gifts can be developed and either used for wrong, or for good, noble and upright

34

plans that are man-made and not God inspired. This is a very important point for our minds can conceive good ideas, but good ideas are not necessarily God ideas. St Benedict, in his chapter on humility, quotes from Proverbs, telling us: 'There are ways that seem right to men that can lead to the depths of hell' (Prov. 16:25). Adam's sin was that he wanted autonomy; many of our ideas can be good, worthy and upright but deep down it can be our independent mind that is the driving force and not the word of God.

Before Jesus went back to the Father, he promised that he would send his Holy Spirit, and one of the Spirit's main works would be to convict the world of sin. I hope your heart does not sink when you read that. I do not intend to make you feel terribly guilty, for that is the work of Satan. He it is who accuses the brethren; it is the Holy Spirit who convicts – that is, convinces us that we are sinners – and he only does this in order to comfort us with the truth that there is a remedy in Jesus Christ. It is good to know that Jesus Christ is the saviour, but we can rush to him begging to be saved from all sorts of troubles and fail to ask to be saved from our sin because we are not aware how sinful we are. We did not become sinners the day we committed our first sin. We were born sinners. Again we go back to the account of the Fall in Genesis in order to recognise in ourselves how much we are sons and daughters of our fallen parents. Sin is our attempt to disown God and stand in independence. We resent our God-origin and wish to have autonomy. If we are honest we will see that trait in ourselves. How frustrating our limitations can become. How annoying it can be to have things go wrong. It is amazing how inanimate objects can seem to take on a life of their own when you are trying to organise them.

Is God's will a delight for me, or is it a duty? Intellectually I can know it is good, but emotionally it is often very demanding and not in line with my wants. For example, we all know that it is good to spend some time in prayer; yet how hard it is actually to get down to it. Thousands of reasons crop up to make us postpone the time. I am the most untidy man that has ever lived; I pray in my room and my room is a tip! Whenever I sit down to pray, the thought comes into my mind: 'Why not tidy your room? Now is a good time. The Lord won't mind if you take ten minutes off.' I am sure you will have experienced something similar. How difficult it can be to settle down and pray. All this shows an inner reluctance to be with God. These attitudes lie deep in us, and even though I am a new creation in Chrst, I can still allow these attitudes to take flesh in some external sin. While I can recognise the wrong action I do as sin, often it is easy to fail to see the sin that lies hidden in my attitude.

We were conceived in sin; that does not mean

our parents' act of generation was sinful – it means we are born in sin, we come into existence as hostile to God. God was meant to be the centre of our being, the purpose of our existence. Because of sin he has become off-centre and we have taken the central place in our lives. Therefore God is viewed with suspicion. His very hands stretched out to save us are seen as hands reaching out to unseat us. How is it that God who is so good, that Jesus who was so merciful and compassionate, are not loved naturally by men and women? There is something that distorts our ideas and thoughts of them. This is sin, and there is nothing we can do of ourselves to alter that. All we can do is to admit honestly that that is our condition; then the Spirit will comfort us and show us how 'God loved the world so much that he gave his only Son, so that everyone who believes in him may not be lost but may have eternal life' (John 3:16).

When we begin to see the enormity of sin, when we can admit to God that we often see him as a rival, when we dare to acknowledge that much of our good work comes from selfish motives, then we are in a blessed place to hear that God has a remedy and that it is tailor-made for us.

3

God's Remedy

God dealt with sin by sending his own Son in a body as physical as any sinful body, and in that body God condemned sin. (Rom. 8:3)

We can acquire knowledge either through experience or through learning. Most of those born into Christian families learn about the gospel through being taught. Much depends upon that early presentation. If you had to tell someone the essence of the gospel, I wonder what you would say?

Very early on I learnt about my faith, and I suppose it is not surprising that some truths appeared more attractive than others. The less attractive ones, either because they were mysterious or unpalatable, got pushed into the background. That God had dealt with human sin through the death of Jesus was certainly something I was taught. Unfortunately the language used to convey this doctrine is not helpful. Expressions such as 'atonement', 'making satisfaction for sin', 'bearing God's punishment' are difficult even for mature adults to understand correctly and for young persons they can be horrific. Because I was already pretty suspicious of God, these ideas were offputting. I imagined that Jesus was trying to placate the Father by his terrible death. Theologically, of course, this is nonsense, as it puts Jesus and the Father at opposing ends – Jesus appears to be bargaining with the angry Father by taking on our sufferings. But it is so near the truth that it can be mistaken for the truth. The whole point is that the Father and Son are working together for our rescue. It is through the Father's mercy that he sends his Son; the Son has not come on his own initiative to appease the angry Father.

The way I came to realise the doctrine of the Cross was gradual and painful. After Vatican II we were encouraged to be ecumenical and I am eternally grateful to Protestant pastors who unknowingly made me rethink my understandings. I began looking at my theology and all that I had been taught, and to my utter joy, I started to discover the same teaching as that of my Protestant friends. I have to admit that it needed digging out, and the language often obscured the truth. I feel sure now that if only someone had spelt out to me, in simple language, what the Cross was about, not just dwelling on the immense sufferings of Christ, rousing pity and regret in me, I would have come to an understanding much earlier. Too frequently we assume everyone has a firm grasp of the meaning of the Cross, and so it does not often get preached about. This can have very serious results, because when people do not see the saving power of the Cross of Christ they will look for other solutions to the problems of their lives.

In this chapter I want to explain as clearly as I can what God has done to reconcile us with himself and to give us new life.

God's desire to heal us

We often have the feeling that if we could just get the political scene right then all our troubles would disappear. You have only to listen to any party political broadcast to see how people do believe that right politics will give the answers to our problems. The other false god which promises solutions is the economy. If we could only get that straight then we would live in peace and prosperity.

But the problem is neither politics nor economics – it lies in the heart of humanity. There is a deep flaw within all human beings. We are extremely talented, yet we are very restless. We can aspire to the heights of heaven, yet we can cause utter hell to ourselves and others. We can do the most noble of deeds and yet also the most foul.

God, in making the human race, made people like himself; therefore we can be quite God-like in some of the things we can do. I am

40

sure we have all experienced those moments when we seem lifted above ourselves. But the human being was not made to be God, only God-like. In trying to snatch to ourselves God-decisions we threw everything out of balance. Hence we experience within ourselves this strange contradiction – nobility and baseness. This is not solved by politics, nor economics, nor self-reform programmes; it is solved by God who so loved the world he had invented and into which he had put himself, that, when it went wrong, he sent his Son to take that wrong into himself and to deal with it as only God could.

May God forgive me, but I used to wonder why Jesus, who talked so much about forgiveness, did not just forgive us our sins and start again. Why all this need for buying back, making reparation and satisfaction? After all, when someone messes up the plans I have made, I can forgive them and say: 'Well, let's have another go.' Clearly, I did not understand that sin needs more than forgiveness – it needs healing. Sin damages the person who commits it. It leaves them wounded and in need of reparation. A healthy eye delights in the light, but if I wilfully damage my eye, then the light becomes painful to it. The light has not changed, it is my eye that has changed and it is my eye that needs repairing. When we sin, we do not damage God, we damage ourselves and as a result we find God's presence painful.

41

We not only need forgiving, but we also need repairing so that we can be in relationship with God again.

God's plan to heal human beings of the effects of sin is truly extraordinary. He decides that one of the sons of Adam should be the rescuer of the human race. But how could that possibly happen, since all born of Adam are born in bondage right from the start? God's plan is that his Son, the second Person of the blessed Trinity, should become a man. He does not become man in the way that Adam was made man; there is no second starting of the human race out of nothing; God's Son is born from one of the daughters of Adam. The child born of Mary truly is a son of man, and therefore he can be a legitimate representative of that race. Mary conceives by the overshadowing of the Holy Spirit, so the child born of her is also a Son of God. A son has been born to the human race who has not lost the illumining light of God's Spirit. There now stands among the sons of men One who is not in bondage.

If you have read *Out of the Silent Planet* and *Perelandra* by C. S. Lewis, you will remember how the 'eldil' and all those other beautiful, shadowy creatures that he described so vividly, were astounded at the rumour that Maledil had visited the silent planet in some humble form. So the Father's plan to send his Son as a man must have given the angels of heaven much food for thought. There are those who believe that is why there was a battle in heaven – some angels refused to submit to such a plan. How could the all-holy, all-wise and all-powerful God enter a lower nature and become limited and need to grow in knowledge? I have often wondered how there could ever be a battle in heaven, but it is beyond the scope of this book to explore such thinking. Alas we have become very familiar with the idea that God became man, we need to pause and wonder at the enormity of such a step. Would we be prepared to become a bee to help the world of bees?

As a young man, I always looked on Jesus as being God dressed up as a man, and because he was God he would therefore know everything. That was why he could read people's minds and know what they were thinking, and that was why he did miracles and knew the answer to tricky questions. Then I read F. X. Durwell's *In the Redeeming Christ*, and that started me on a long journey of reassessing my idea of how much of a man Jesus really became. I began asking things like: did Jesus ask a genuine question when the woman touched the hem of his garment and he said: 'Who touched me?' It is difficult to answer that because as God he should know but as man he would not, unless he was a superman or a pseudo-man. Also when he was a boy being taught the skills of carpentry by Joseph, was he standing there with his arms folded saying to himself: 'I actually created the universe' or was he a little boy learning? Today, when people hear about Jesus they discover very early on that he was God and although they are told that he was also a man, the God part overshadows the human part and we find it very difficult to think of him as a man like ourselves. Those who lived with him had no doubt that he was a man; they shared his daily life and they saw him eat, grow tired and need to sleep. They had to make the difficult journey of learning that he was God. I have found tremendous comfort in thinking of Jesus standing where I stand asking questions and having to make decisions. Clearly he 'grew in wisdom' as Scripture tells us, and through the working of the Holy Spirit he came to know who he was and what his mission was. He could not cease to be God but he seems to have renounced the privileges of his position and entered into the nature of humanity so that he could wrestle with Satan, the conqueror of the human race, as a man.

> His state was divine,
> yet he did not cling
> to his equality with God
> but emptied himself
> to assume the condition of a slave,
> and he became as men are,
> and being as all men are,
> he was humbler yet,
> even to accepting death,
> death on a cross. (Phil. 2:6–8)

44

God's Remedy

God's plan is that a man should conquer the one who conquered humans and to make this possible he sent his Son to become a man. By living in human nature and not according to it, Jesus began to overcome the enemy of the human race. Here was a son of Adam who was not living as a son of Adam. He did only the will of the Father. Jesus is doing what the first Adam failed to do; he is living not according to his own ideas, but on 'every word that comes from the mouth of God'. Here is the Christ, the anointed One, who lives by the guiding of the Spirit. He does this in a fallen world and in a fallen nature. He comes to meet the enemy with a nature that is wounded and weak, and with that equipment he takes up the battle.

Since all the children share the same blood and flesh, he too shared equally in it, so that by his death he could take away all the power of the devil, who had power over death, and set free all those who had been held in slavery all their lives by the fear of death. For it was not the angels that he took to himself; he took to himself descent from Abraham. It was essential that he should in this way become completely like his brothers so that he could be a compassionate and trustworthy high priest of God's religion, able to atone for human sins. That is, because he has himself been through temptation he is able to help others who are tempted. (Heb. 2:14–18)

For it is not as if we had a high priest who was incapable of feeling our weaknesses with us; but we have one who has been tempted in every way that we are, though he is without sin. (Heb. 4:15)

The sinless One, having come into a world where there was sin and having adopted a nature wounded by sin, now became accessible to the evil one who relentlessly attacked him since he saw him as a threat to his hold over the sons and daughters of Adam. It is not surprising that Jesus, after hearing the confirming words at his baptism 'You are my beloved Son in whom I am well pleased', should have been tempted in the desert with the very words: '*If* you are the Son of God, tell these stones to turn into loaves.' One of our race conquers Satan, the prince of this world, by living as a man in this world, yet never submitting to the dictates of him who ruled all people.

Another way that Jesus conquers Satan is by unseating him from his position as prince of this world. When Adam and Eve, who were made to be masters here on earth, submitted to Satan's deception, Satan became the ruler. In his public life Jesus attacks Satan in all the places where he has taken up his abode as lord. For this work he needed the anointing of the Holy Spirit so that he could confront the evil one. When Jesus was accused of casting out evil spirits by the power of Beelzebul, the prince of devils, he retorted that it was through the power of the Holy Spirit that he did such things: 'If it is through the Spirit of God that I cast devils out, then know that the kingdom of God has overtaken you' (Matt. 12:28).

The kingdom of God is not a geographical place – it is anywhere where God's rule is carried out. Jesus has come to restore God's rule on earth; so every time he meets the evil one pretending to be in charge, Jesus shows who is the master by commanding Satan to depart. I think that rather curious verse about binding the strong man first before you can plunder his house, refers to the fact that Jesus has come to bind Satan so that he can win back what rightfully belongs to the Father: 'How can anyone make his way into a strong man's house and burgle his property unless he has tied up the strong man first? Only then can he burgle his house' (Matt. 12:29). Every time Jesus meets the strong one exercising his unlawful authority he drives him out. The gospel stories are full of people being delivered from the power of the devil.

In his public life Jesus healed the sick, thus showing that he did not see sickness as part of the kingdom of God. I have heard people mistakenly saying to the sick: 'Well, it is God's will.' True, it is his permissive will, but not his direct will. If it is God's express will, then why did Jesus heal the sick, and how can we justify our going to hospitals and doctors, if God should want us sick? Clearly, it is not God's direct will that we should be sick. God can, of course, use sickness and draw good from it; but that does not make sickness a good thing in itself. Quite simply, sickness is an evil. This does not mean that a sick person is evil; it means that they are being afflicted by evil. Jesus came to re-establish God's rule here on earth and so whenever he meets evil in any form he comes against it showing who the rightful Master is. The kingdom of God is not yet here amongst us in all its glory but because it has already begun here on earth, we see it now and then breaking through into the present. Healings do still happen today.

To be prince of this world is a very high title so we should not be surprised if this prince should be able to use things of this world for his purpose. If I say that the storm which broke onto the boat the Lord was sleeping in was demon caused, I do not then mean that all bad weather is demon instigated. The evil one can use things of this earth for his reasons; the Lord overrules his commands showing that he is the Lord of the earth.

So Jesus overcame the evil one by living in flesh yet never submitting to the one who had conquered flesh. He also overcame by ousting the usurper from the places where he had taken up his abode. But all these victories only affect the person Jesus; he is living a human life free of sin but this does not free the race from sin.

God's Remedy

When Jesus heals a sick person, it is Jesus who
conquers the sickness; the sick person remains
vulnerable to further attacks. We must now
look at the main reason for Jesus becoming a
man. This is the whole purpose of his coming
among us and dying and rising to a new life.

Jesus' death and resurrection

I always found it very difficult to understand
why Jesus had to die. Somehow it made me
fear the Father who, in some way, was placated
and satisfied by this terrible death. I could not
see how death could blot out sin; I could not
see why Jesus had to die for my sin, and, if his
death took away my sins, how was it that I still
sinned? All these thoughts troubled me and
made me uneasy about this part of Christianity.
I could feel attracted to the God of nature, I
could find interest in books on prayer, I wanted
to live a spiritual life. I was drawn to the goodness of the Lord – but all talk about sacrifice
and atonement was very strange and mysti-
fying. I have given an immense amount of time
and effort in searching into this mystery and
only gradually, and very gradually, has it begun
to yield light. Here in the sunset of my life I
think I have begun to grasp its meaning. I hope
I can share some of this with you using the
simplest ideas I can find. It would be very
appropriate if you paused at this moment and

49

asked the Holy Spirit to lead you into an understanding of his truth.

If it was winter, and we were standing around a huge bonfire in the Arctic Circle, then, if anyone should turn away from the fire and walk off, they would go into the dark and the cold. It would not be the bonfire putting them in the dark and cold, it would be the consequence of their choice to turn and walk away from the source of light and heat. When we sin, we choose something other than God. We turn away from the One who is the source of life and goodness. To turn away from that which gives life, is to turn towards that which will not give life. The non-life that follows is a consequence of our choice. It is not God punishing us with death; rather he is saying: 'If you leave me, the source of life, then there is no alternative. Even I cannot prevent the result from happening. I, and I alone, am the One who gives life.' When I began to look at God's punishment for sin as a consequence of sin, I started to see the word 'punishment' in a new way. I realised that it was right and just that such serious consequences should follow turning one's back on God. Of course I am talking here about responsible sin. Adam and Eve's sin was very responsible and deliberate. They chose not to live by God, but by their own decisions. The result was that they lost their ability to know God in their spirit; they could now only speculate about him in their minds. Here was a major disaster; God's special creature was now unable to know him and to die in that state would mean eternal separation from him.

Darkness and light cannot be together. If you have a dark room and you bring light into it, the darkness has to go. Notice that you cannot bring darkness into a lighted room, you can only remove the light and the darkness will return. This just shows that light is stronger than darkness. Let us apply the same principle to a deeper truth. Evil and God cannot be in relationship. God made the human being good. God wanted to have relationship with men and women so he created them in his own image and likeness. But the human race did evil and made it impossible to remain in relationship with God. However, God loves people, so he comes up with a remedy. He sends his Son to become a man, and we have seen above that he really became a man. There is no sin in him for it was through the Holy Spirit that he took flesh. Here is the man that God intended Adam to be. The incredible plan of the Father is that this beloved Son of his should take on himself the sins of humanity. The Son willingly consents to this. Jesus did not sin but he allowed in some way all the sins of the human race to be loaded onto him and he experienced the consequences of sin – separation from the source of life, namely death. Scripture goes very far in

51

describing this for it says: 'God made the sinless one into sin' (2 Cor. 5:21).

Just imagine what a cost that was for Jesus. He, who spent himself in doing the Father's will, now felt himself removed from the Father. He would have experienced the justice of God being worked out on him for the very nature of God makes it impossible for sin and God to be in relationship. The physical agony of crucifixion is terrible, but for Jesus to experience the separation from the Father caused by our sins, is something we can hardly begin to fathom. The cry 'Why have you forsaken me?' took on for me an awful meaning when I began to see Jesus was bearing the justice of God in my place. What must the cost have been to the Father to see his righteous judgement carried out on his Son? God the Father spared Abraham that sacrifice but he willingly gave us his own Son.

But why was all this necessary? Here we must try to understand God's extraordinary plan. Because Jesus was God, every action of his would have infinite value. Therefore when he took on himself the consequences of our sins, he would have met those consequences to the full. The result of sin was that the human race was incapable of having relationship with God and was unable to know God's will, and thus unable to fulfil it. That barrier was now removed, because Jesus' death had such infinite value that death, real death, was no longer due

to those who belonged to Christ. So, by
entering into death, Jesus paid the full debt for
sin. He did not pretend to die, he actually died;
he bore the debt completely.

Thus the death of Jesus has been the means
by which our sins are forgiven. Earlier we saw
that the healing of sin requires more than
forgiveness – for, after all, forgiveness does not
save us from sinning again; we need in some
way to be set free from sinning. In dying Jesus
met the demands of sin, but when he entered
into death, an innocent man entered into the
region where only sinners go. The kingdom of
death has no right or power to keep captive
anyone who had never sinned. When Jesus paid
the full debt for sin by dying, death could not
keep hold of him so he broke out of the bonds
of death and returned to his body, causing it to
rise to new life. The resurrection does not mean
that Jesus came back to life in the same way
that Lazarus did; no, he rose to a new life.
Here was a son of Adam, now totally and
utterly freed from the bondages of Adam. Here
was the conqueror of Satan, who could never
be personally attacked again, save through the
members of his body still living on earth. Here
was the new Adam and from him a new race
would spring. Those born from the old Adam
can have a new birth through water and the
Holy Spirit into this new Adam. This new race
would still dwell on earth in the fallen world,
but by their daily choosing to live in the new

life that they have received, they could escape from the old Adam way. The new life that they are called to live is not in the realm of feeling, nor in the realm of experience in the sense of experience leading to faith; rather it is in the realm of faith which will lead to experience. It is interesting to see how often Jesus said to those who were healed by him, 'It is your faith that has set you free'.

When I began to see all this with my inner eye, then familiar gospel texts took on a new meaning. Words such as 'I am the Way, the Truth and the Life' suddenly made immense sense. I understood now that there was no way to heaven save through being united to Jesus Christ. I saw Christianity as a process of being 'Christed', of being transformed into the One who had a right to go to the Father. What a terrible tragedy it is when Christianity is seen as rules and regulations whereby we merit our way into heaven. Jesus has told us, 'There is no way to the Father save through me'. This does not make it all easy; our self-will rebels against depending on another. If someone offers us a gift, it does not become ours until we accept it, take hold of it, unwrap it and use it. Christ has done something immense for us, and he is forever holding out to us this gift of new life in him. The spiritual path is the art of living that new life.

4

Gifts Have to be Received

Unless a wheat grain falls on the ground and dies, it remains only a single grain; but if it dies, it yields a rich harvest. (John 12:24)

I wonder if you have ever prepared a gift, gone to quite a lot of trouble over it, and had it hardly noticed when you gave it? I remember once making someone a Christmas card. I took a great deal of care, wrote a special text on it, and sent it off with excitement and some expectation. I got a card back, which I suppose was an acknowledgement because I do not think this person would ordinarily have sent me one, but absolutely no reference was made to my own card. The disappointment was really quite deep. If we feel hurt when others fail to appreciate what we do for them, imagine how much more we must hurt God when we refuse to accept the gift he is offering us in his Son.

Gifts need both to be given *and* received before they can properly be called our own. Unless we unwrap and use what we have been given, we do not profit by the gift. If I am thirsty and am given a cool drink, I am not refreshed until I drink what I have been given. So also, it is not enough to know what God has done for me through his Son; I need to appropriate his gift, and this is a lifetime's job. If a lemon branch is grafted onto an orange tree, and the graft takes, then we have a very interesting situation – we have a lemon branch with orange life entering into it. Not being a botanist I do not know what fruit will be produced, but the point of the illustration is that the lemon branch is now living with a new kind of life, and that new life has to be continually accepted if the fruit is going to be produced; if ever it rejected that new life, then the branch would die.

In the last chapter we looked at what Jesus Christ was doing for us by dying and rising from the dead. We tried to see what he did. In this chapter we want to look at how his dying and rising affect us.

Before Jesus went back to his Father, he promised that after he had gone the Holy Spirit would be sent: 'I shall ask the Father, and he will give you another Advocate to be with you for ever' (John 14:16).

In the first Letter of St John, Jesus is referred to as our advocate with the Father (2:1–2). An advocate is someone who pleads the cause of another in the court of law. It is comforting to know that Jesus is at the right hand of the Father making intercession for us. So, when

Jesus tells us that we will have 'another Advocate', does that mean we will now have two intercessors in heaven? In the text quoted above we are told that this new Advocate will 'be with us for ever', and in John 14:26 we learn that he will teach us everything and remind us of all that Jesus has said. He has come to plead the cause of Jesus with us. This is the main reason for God sending the Holy Spirit. He comes so that he may work on all, prompting, guiding, leading and causing everyone to question and search for the reasons of life. The Holy Spirit is not confined to believers; he is forever prompting, nudging, using every situation for his purposes. Not all of us have been able to meet Jesus in the flesh; the Spirit of God has been sent to challenge everyone born into this world, confronting them with the One who has risen from the dead. He deals with us as individuals, never forcing but also never desisting.

In the last chapter we saw how Jesus' death dealt with our actual sins, and how his resurrection enables us to live a new life, whereby we need not sin. For years I found it very difficult to see how Jesus' death could cancel my sins and remove the barrier between me and God. My understanding was blocked because the doctrine of atonement seemed to portray an angry God who could only be placated by a blood sacrifice. These wrong ideas of God seemed to be confirmed for me by the fact that the Old Testament was full of blood sacrifices.

This ignorance virtually meant that I did not take hold of what Jesus had done by his death and resurrection since I could not accept a God, who was meant to be good, acting in what appeared to be such a cruel way. In other words false ideas about God were successfully preventing me from putting my faith and trust in those very things he had done to save me. I do not think that I consciously rejected the doctrine of atonement, but rather I consigned it to the realm of mystery, and I vaguely hoped my understanding of it was wrong.

This leads me to see how important it is to try to understand the gospel and not just to believe it. Certainly it is more important to believe than to understand, but we can often be prevented from having a healthy belief because of some misunderstanding. Faith is beyond reason, not contrary to it. Thank God that today the Church is refinding her mission to teach and explain. All over the country small study groups are springing up.

This, alas, can produce a different kind of problem. People can mistake understanding for believing. That brings me back to my illustration about the accepting of gifts. It is not enough to know that Jesus has borne my sins; I must act on that truth. Fear and anxiety about our sins can plague us, and Satan will certainly cash in on such tendencies by trying to convince us that we will not receive forgiveness. This is where strong, determined action is required.

God's revelation to us is that his Son has borne our sins, and it is on that truth that we must direct our lives. When Jesus took our sins and died for them, this act of his had infinite value because he is God, and so all that blocks a sinner from God has now been removed. My sins, your sins, and even all the sins yet to be committed, have been dealt with. This does not mean that universal pardon has been applied to all; it means that there is pardon for all who will go to collect it. This involves admitting my sin; for I cannot receive pardon for something that I do not admit to. When we confess our sins, Jesus says to his Father: 'Father, I have dealt with that.' It is then the Spirit's work to apply the saving death and rising of Jesus to the sinner. That is why the Holy Spirit is known as the sanctifier – he is constantly applying the healing, saving work of Jesus to those who humbly ask for it. Needless to say, this does not give us the liberty to sin and then claim the forgiveness won by Christ, because genuine confession of sin requires regret and repentance.

Standing on the truth that Christ has borne our sins does not mean that we try to feel this truth. We are not asked to work up our emotions or feelings; we are simply asked to accept the truth of God's word. This requires discipline; it means denying our anxieties, our arguments, our fears. We have to stand deliberately on what God has said. This is what it

means to live by the Spirit. We take the words
that God has spoken and we trust in their promise and refuse to be blown about by every
wind.

New life

Sin needs more than forgiveness; it needs
taking away. We are weak, and although we
may regret our actions and ask forgiveness, this
does not stop us from committing that sin again.
Now we must try to understand how the resurrection of Christ is our hope of living a new
life.

Jesus took to himself the nature of Adam,
but he never lived according to its demands. In
his obedience to his Father, he was overcoming
the one who had overcome the human race.
Here was one of the sons of Adam conquering
the conqueror of the sons of Adam. Jesus spent
his life dying to the human nature he had taken
to himself. On Calvary, he died in fact to that
nature. He laid it down. When the Father
raised him to life, he did not bring him back to
the life he had laid down; he raised him to a
new life, a life inaccessible to evil, a life that
was powerful, a life that made him Lord with
a right to reign on earth and in heaven. Mani-
festly the Jesus who kept appearing to his disciples after he had risen was very different from
the Jesus they had walked the roads with in

Galilee. Yet the person was the same; he was still man, but he was transcendent, risen, new.

The plan of the Father is to have this new life transmitted to the children of Adam. Life comes through birth, so how can these children of Adam receive this life since they have already been born? They must be born again, Jesus said. This new birth is accomplished through water and the Holy Spirit. God's plan is not to reform the Adam life; his plan is to do away with it. It must die and be replaced by this new life of the risen Christ. St Paul teaches us that when we were baptised, we were baptised into the death of Christ, so that we could imitate him in his resurrection. This was clearly demonstrated in the old rite of baptism – the going under the water signified the dying and burial, the coming up the rising to new life in Christ.

How important it is to understand that new life is *new life*. It is not our old life enhanced, improved, renovated. It is something new. It is the act of believing what God has done for us through the death and resurrection of his Son that makes the work of Jesus effective in us. Any ignorance as to what has been done, can render God's saving power inoperative in us. Any thinking that the new life we have received is only old life improved can successfully block the power of the Cross from having its effect in our lives. Again how important it is for us to know and understand what God has done for us so that we can put our faith in his action. Ignorance is the best way of rendering the gospel impotent, for it is faith that activates the power of God, and when there is ignorance as to what God has done, then acts of faith cannot be made.

I meet people today whose understanding of the Christian faith is something as follows:

> Jesus came to teach us what to do. He told us to love God, to love our neighbour, even love our enemy. He told us not to lie, cheat or be unfair. To sum up, he told us to be good. His teachings were not popular, so they did away with him by nailing him to a cross. To prove to all that he was God, he rose from the dead. This makes his teachings very important and our lives will be judged on how well we have put his teachings into practice. Hopefully after we die we will hear: 'Well done, good and faithful servant, enter into the kingdom prepared for you and the angels'.

There is much truth in this and that is what makes it all the more deceptive. The death of Jesus is just seen as a regrettable event, which really need not have happened; so the faith called for by such teaching stretches only to the fact that Jesus was God and therefore his teaching must be sound. There is no call for faith in what Jesus did by dying and rising again, and that cuts at the very root of the

62

gospel. When faith is not centred on the main act of the gospel, the death and resurrection of the Lord, then the power of the Cross is blocked. People who believe this version of the gospel may be very nice, respectable, law-abiding citizens, but is it new life that they are living or old life improved?

We must not imagine that we can do nothing with our natural life. We can learn to mask our real self. We can smile when we would rather not; we can look calm when in fact we are agitated; appear welcoming when we are bored. Respectability can mask itself as Christianity. A nice church, nice people, a nice service – all very decent, proper and right.

As a novice, I was expected to spend some time each day in personal prayer. This took place at a certain time and one was expected to be there. But your presence did not mean you actually prayed. You may have looked prayerful, recollected, even holy, but that could have all been external. This raises a very serious question: how do we learn to live by this new life that is in us? Do we just sit around hoping that one day it will take over? This question has bothered me for a long time and I have given years of thought to it. It first presented itself to me in this form: 'If I have new life in me and I am a new creation, how is it that I still sin?' At first I began to think along the lines, 'I am not yet a new creation; hopefully one day I will be', but that is to deny Scripture

63

which clearly says: For anyone who is in Christ, there is a new creation; the old creation has gone, and now the new one is here' (2 Cor. 5:17).

Shoddy thinking, imagining that new life is only old life dusted up, successfully stops us making an act of faith in the truth that Jesus has won us new life. We must stand on what God has told us and not on what we either feel or experience. I am beginning to understand that new life cannot be lived by muscle, but that it grows in us as we call on its power to be in our lives. I believe it is very deliberate acts of trust that the power of the Cross is greater than the power of sin in me which make this life grow. Our faith needs exercising. Once we are in Christ, we have a new life, and that life has to grow and develop. A healthy new-born baby has a full human body. There is nothing more to be added – all is there; but it needs development and growth; it has to learn how to use all its various parts. So, too, with this new life in Christ; it is all there, but it needs to grow and develop, and we have to learn how to use it. Once we begin to think it is not there, but is something yet to come to us, then we are not accepting in faith what Jesus has done, because we do not believe he has done it. If I deny that I already have new life, then I virtually paralyse that new life.

What makes it so difficult to live this new life is that there is no new set of muscles to use. I wonder what you do when you see someone approaching whom you do not like? (Note that God does not command us to like everyone; he commands us to love them, and that is quite different.) We can begin by calling on our natural powers to be nice. We can even smile and say the right things. We may even deceive the person and then they stay longer than we expected and sooner or later they will touch a soft spot and we blow our stack. Then we go away from that encounter angry with the person, angry with ourselves and making resolutions that next time we will succeed. But surely we are right to assume that some effort must be made on our part, especially if we have never yet experienced the new life taking over. I do not believe that it is wrong to put on a smile and to do our best, provided we know that this is not the real thing. However our first action must be to declare that the power of the Cross is greater than the power of unlove in us. Having called on God, we then offer him our poor effort. As our trust in the power of the Cross grows through the Holy Spirit's teaching and through our praise and thanks to God, we will begin to experience its reality in our lives. Larry Christenson, an American Lutheran pastor, gave this illustration: he said that if you want to build a concrete archway, you first make a wooden form for the arch. It is not the arch itself, only a form into which the concrete must be poured. Once the concrete has set, the

65

wooden form is taken away. Our small acts of charity are only the wooden form – they are not the real thing. We offer them to God and ask him to pour into our efforts the real thing. In time he will.

Our task is not to overcome, but to allow Jesus to overcome in us. We are not called to fight with our own power, but to fight with the power of the risen Christ. In the Letter to the Ephesians (6:10) we are told 'to grow strong' not with our own power but 'with the strength of his power'. This does not mean that there is no effort on our part; our effort is to use Christ. If you row a boat, then the boat moves by your power. When you sail a boat it is moved by the power of the wind, but you have to cooperate with the wind. Holiness is not something that we achieve; it is something that God achieves in us if we will let him. All our efforts are to allow the work of Jesus to become effective in us.

Another reason why it is so difficult to live by this new life is quite simply the fact that we do not want to live by it. Deep down in all of us is the originating sin, the sin that says, 'I'll do it on my own. I'll manage; I do not need help'. It is the sin of Adam when he said: 'I'll go my own way. I'll think it out. I am intelligent.' We were created to be God-centred; sin has made us self-centred. We find it very hard to accept salvation as a gift; we would like to be able to take some credit. Naaman resisted doing what the prophet Elisha told him to do. He had hoped that he would be asked to perform a noble, heroic deed, so that he could claim some credit for his healing (2 Kings 5). This drive is deep within us all; even our desire to serve God and do what is right can spring from our ambition to be thought good. We can do what is expected of us for wrong reasons. Man-made goodness has something unattractive about it. It is hard to describe, but deep down we recognise it – it is just too good, too right. Genuine holiness is awe-inspiring and makes us want to give God the praise for what he can do in our sin-prone nature.

Scripture refers to our death in Christ both as something already achieved and as something yet to be accomplished. We read:

All those who belong to Christ Jesus have crucified self with all its passions and desires. (Gal. 5:24 *New Jerusalem Bible*)

We must realise that our former selves have been crucified with him to destroy this sinful body and to free us from the slavery of sin. (Rom. 6:6)

All that is very definite and final, yet we also read:

That is why you must kill everything in you that belongs only to earthly life: fornication, impurity, guilty passion, evil desires . . . (Col. 3:5)

67

But if by the Spirit you put an end to the
misdeeds of the body you will live.
(Rom. 8:13)

We must remember that we can live our lives
on many levels. We can be controlled by our
bodies, our souls or by what the Spirit of God
reveals to us. Whatever choice we make it is
not a once-and-for-all decision. If we choose to
live by the Spirit, constantly we have to
continue to make that choice. Just as when
someone decides to sing a song, they have to
continue in that choice until the end of the
song. It is not a matter of feeling. Daily we
have to choose to live the new life we have
received. Daily we need to believe that the
power of the Cross is greater than any other
power we may encounter. We will not feel this
truth; we may not even experience it, but
experiences must not direct our lives. This does
not mean that experiences are not important.
The Church I grew up in was very suspicious
of them, and I think I now understand the
reason why. To believe something because I
experience it, is not very sound. Very often I
experience God as absent, far-away, remote
and if I allow these feelings to influence me, I
will feel low and abandoned. Sometimes,
though not often, I feel God is present, but that
does not make him present; he is always present
because he has said so. Thus to base my life on
my experiences would be very unwise. But if I

trust in God's promises, I will experience his fidelity – that sort of experience is good and right and should be expected.

The kingdom of God is not here in all its fullness. We are in an unique period in history, where the enemy has been defeated but is not yet chained up. Scripture tells us that he roars around like a lion, but we must resist him, strong in faith (1 Peter 5:8–9). We have received the first-fruits of the Spirit in our own spirit: 'The Spirit himself and our spirit bear united witness that we are children of God' (Rom. 8:16). But our own bodies are not yet redeemed: ' . . . we too groan inwardly as we wait for our bodies to be set free' (Rom. 8:23).

So already we are a new creation, yet we have to continue to make the choice to live as such. Only experience can teach us that if we live on the level of the Spirit and are directed by him, then we will be set free. Reason finds it very difficult to grasp this, and the western world is largely mind-controlled.

God has told us that we can have, or do have, new life in Christ. The more we exercise our belief in this fact and endeavour to live by its message, the more we will experience the power of the risen Lord in us. As this new life grows in us, so our actions will begin to be new as well. The battle lies in the decision who is going to control our minds?

5

The God Who Speaks

Where were you when I laid the earth's
*   foundations?*
Tell me, since you are so well-informed!
Who decided the dimensions of it, do you
*   know?*
Or who stretched the measuring line across
*   it?*
What supports its pillars at their bases?
Who laid its cornerstone
when all the stars of the morning were singing
*   with joy,*
and the Sons of God in chorus were chanting
*   praise?* (Job 38:4–7)

There is a battle going on for our mind.
Whoever, or whatever, controls that, controls
us. Our bodily desires can control us, or our
own thinking can be our master, or we can
allow the Holy Spirit to direct and guide us.
The choice is ours. But we were born with a
nature biased towards self rather than God, and
we find a battle raging within us. St Augustine
wrote that 'Our hearts are restless until they

rest in Thee' – alas, we imagine that restlessness can be assuaged by self-gratification, and this is the deception at the very root of our being; what cannot be totally satisfying appears to be so, and what God offers, which is our only way of hope, seems to our jaundiced eyes to be stony, threatening and unprofitable.

The question I want to wrestle with in this chapter is how do we allow the Holy Spirit to control our thinking? The obvious answer is to read Scripture where God reveals himself and his plans to us. While I agree that the word of God is of utmost importance, I have to question if it is not too simplistic to expect that anyone will discover God just by reading his word. Long before we open the Bible or have it opened to us, we have already formed a picture of God. This picture can come through a chance remark, through a feeling of awe or fear felt in a strange place, or through saying some prayer for a desperate need that, apparently, was not answered.

I know someone who had a deep-rooted fear of God. It was not hard to trace from where that fear came – a domineering father had so destroyed the idea 'father' that when God was described in this way a terrible picture was conceived. As I say it was fairly easy to see where the problem came from, but it was no simple job to erase that first impression. This man was not well versed in Scripture and I wanted him to meet the merciful Lord who

71

forgave sinners and healed the sick. But my advice to read Scripture was disastrous for it only confirmed his fear of God. Every passage where Jesus was speaking to the Pharisees and correcting them, my friend took to himself; every act of mercy carried out by the Lord, he saw as being done to those who in some sense were worthy. This image that my friend had of God overrode everything that Scripture was trying to say. He was not able to hear the truth and even when I pointed out how illogical he was – for it says clearly that Jesus came for sinners – he just could not believe that this applied to him. This shows how important early ideas of God are and how easy it is to pick up false impressions.

I wonder if you have had the experience of seeing a film of a novel you once read? Often I have been disappointed by the way a favourite character was portrayed. On going back to the book and checking carefully how the author described this person, I have discovered that I had taken liberties and had imagined the person as I wanted them to be and not as the author was describing them. None of us has seen God and therefore we are tempted to form our own idea of him and this idea can be quite contrary to what God has said about himself. Once we have formed our picture, it will leap in and colour our thinking every time we hear the word 'God'.

I feel that it is very important for these

pictures of God to be exposed to the light. We can be frightened even to admit to ourselves what we really feel about God. We have been told that he is perfect, all-good and all-merciful, and we can so easily trot out these answers when we are questioned about him. But we need to be desperately honest here and ask, 'Is God good in my eyes? Is he someone I can trust absolutely, or is he someone I know I ought to trust?' Too often the God we harbour in the depths of our being bears little or no resemblance to the picture Jesus drew of the Father when he told us the parable of the pro-digal son.

My early impressions of God, picked up somewhere in childhood, had so coloured my ideas of God, that no matter what was said about him, these deep-rooted notions rendered every new picture invalid, ineffective and unconvincing. It was not a conscious process, it was a pattern of thinking that I had fallen into. I never dared to share those pictures I had of God with anyone; I feared they would be thought blasphemous. I now see how important it is to bring these shadowy thoughts out into the full light of day. When they remain in the unconscious, they are indistinct, obscure, fuzzy and unclear. St Paul urged: '. . . every thought is our prisoner, captured to be brought into obedience to Christ' (2 Cor. 10:4–5).

To be wrong about God is to be wrong about everything. Hence there is a serious battle to

73

control our minds. So how do we begin to get a true picture of God? That is not an easy question to answer. I think we can be helped by looking at how we get to know people. It is not enough just to hear them speak, we need to watch them, see how they behave, how they handle things, are they true to their word? Are they moody, gentle, thoughtful? Slowly we begin to piece together a picture. So it must be with God. We need to tune into all the ways he speaks with us. I needed to reconcile the God of the fields with the God I met in church. I am sure that if I had understood that the God who spoke to me in church was the same as the One I met in the woods, I would have listened with a different attitude.

How important it is to find a wise guide to walk with us as we set out on this pilgrimage. Alas, parents, who should have been our first guides, often fought shy of the job, and those early impressionable years were lost. This has meant that schools have often had to build on foundations that were not there. How good it would have been if someone had confirmed for me that what I contacted in sunshine, colour, or in the bold sweep of hills, was a glimmer of him who dances in the skies. What a tragedy it was that the God of church was so forbidding. Before he ever opened his mouth, I felt condemned; hence I dreaded to hear what he had to say.

As we look at the various ways God speaks

74

to us we must remember that no idea I have of God *is* God, and no idea that you have of God *is* God. Therefore our ideas of him are in constant need of change. We are tempted to wrap him up in definitions, tie him down to our human concepts, box him up in our doctrines. How right it is that God should forever burst out of these confines, shatter our images and make us realise he is greater than our wildest thoughts.

When we get to know people we learn about them through all sorts of different channels. We can discover a lot just by seeing how they behave, the way they touch things, how they walk; all these things can convey to us certain insights. So, too, it is with God; simply looking at the things he has made can tell me much about him. What manner of being must he be who can create colour, sunshine, water? Take water; it is such ordinary stuff, yet really it is such extraordinary stuff. It has no colour, no odour, no shape, but it is terribly real. You can ski right across the top of it. It washes, refreshes, gives life, takes it away. What must he be like who invented it, and so much of it? How important it is to take time to look and see and wonder. Try to imagine the world as a black and white photograph – then, hopefully, you will become aware of colour. What must he be like who could think up red, blue, yellow?

We need to take time to listen to the breathing of the world around us. Those of us

who live in vast cities have cut ourselves off
from the wonder of nightfall, the rising of the
sun, the subtle change in seasons. All of us,
wherever we are, are often so absorbed in our
own worlds that we fail to notice the beauty of
nature. As I mentioned earlier, I used to live
and teach in the USA, and there the colours of
the leaves in autumn are much more rich and
remarkable than in Britain. One day, as I was
walking towards the gym with a young student,
I noticed the marvellous greens, yellows and
reds of the leaves on the trees, and I said to
the student, 'Look at that! Isn't it wonderful!'
He became interested but could not discover
what I was looking at and begged me to tell
him. I teased him for a while and then finally
told him I was referring to the leaves. 'Oh,' he
said with obvious disappointment, 'is that all?'

Even our learning can take the mystery out
of life -- rain is no longer God providing the
earth with its needed refreshment, it is just
moisture gathered off the sea, now cooling and
falling as rain. We do a sort of violence to
the seasons by producing daffodils in autumn,
chrysanthemums in spring and strawberries at
Christmas. This, of course, is not wrong and I
find it difficult to say why it makes me uneasy.
But there are some so-called advances in knowledge which are actually harmful and which
prove us to be poor stewards of our world.
Insecticides that poison birds and remove some
species, thus producing an imbalance in nature,

seem to me to show a very uncaring attitude towards God's wonderful creation. In our greed for profit we over-fish the seas, we over-produce crops; we export western techniques to poorer countries and destroy ancient cultures and valued ways of living, all in the name of prosperity. We are not lords of the earth in the sense that we can do with it what we wish. We are co-workers with the One who made it all and invited us to share in its development.

So, God speaks to us through the world around us. All the beauty that I see in creation must in some way be in him who made it. We should strive to think of him in new ways, we should try to break out of our stereotyped manner of speaking with him. Perhaps we should address him as 'the One who makes the rainbows', or as 'the One who listens to the hills', and thus begin to form a new picture, a picture of awe and beauty to replace our dull and faded images.

God also speaks to us through the world within us. If I can get excited over a tree in full flower, how much more ought I to get excited over the God who invented you and me! Alas, not many of us were taught to love ourselves in the correct way. I have found it helpful to think of God forever continuing to create me. A song exists only as long as the singer continues to sing it. We only exist because God chooses to continue singing us into being. How important it is to appreciate the fact that we are alive solely because someone wishes it that way. What a gift it is to see, to hear, to be able to come and go, to touch things, to feel the rough and the smooth. I remember once trying to experience what it was like to be blind. I put my hands over my eyes, but I could still see light seeping through my fingers. One day I actually got into a room where no chink of light penetrated, but in some way I saw, I saw dark. Later on someone told me that to experience what it is to be blind all you have to do is to look in your left shoe with your left foot. You do not see black, you just do not see!

We need to have a healthy appreciation of ourselves and our gifts. Clearly, self-boasting and arrogance are wrong, but it is equally wrong to despise oneself and to consider oneself an unfortunate mistake. Much harm was done in the past in the name of humility, and we need to find a right balance. Who has ever plumbed the mystery of their own being? Or who has understood the subtle moods that come and go like clouds in a summer sky? Who has not asked the question, 'Just who am I?', and not sensed a certain unseating of oneself as an answer is sought? Hopefully all these searchings bring us face to face with the One who tells us from all eternity that he has chosen us to be.

Also what a privilege it is to be allowed to see into the wonder of another person. I remember when a young boy called Mark shared something of himself. He told me that he liked to catch frogs. I thought this a rather interesting thing for a child to want to do and so I asked him all about it. He began to tell me about the tremendous excitement and sense of adventure he felt as he set out to look for frogs, and about the lovely smell of the marshes as he approached the pond. And I asked him: 'Surely when you get to the pond the frogs aren't sitting there waiting for you? How do you catch them?' He said: 'Oh no, of course they've all gone back into the pool as soon as they've heard me coming.'

'Well, what do you do about it?'

'I get right to the edge of the pond and then I stand there, and I pretend I'm a tree.'

'Well yes, that's lovely, but what happens?'

'Well, I may have to stay a very long time, but if I keep very still it may be that the surface of the pond breaks and two eyes will look out. And if I'm lucky, but it doesn't often happen, they may come out and they may sit on the smooth stones within my reach.'

Of course, now I'm caught up in the story and I want to know what's going to happen, so I ask him to tell me more. 'If they do come within my reach, then of course I have to make my move and suddenly I will make a lunge.'

'And do you ever catch them?'

'Oh very rarely.'

'And what happens if you do?'

79

'Ah well, that's the whole triumph. I've caught my frog!'

'And what do you do with him?'

'Oh, I tickle him under the chin and I like to feel his slimy skin, and I envy him because he doesn't go to school.'

'And then what?'

'I let him go.'

You can imagine the frog sinking back into the green pool thinking, 'What was all that about?' But it's not the frog I'm interested in; it's the little boy. By telling me what he liked to do, he told me a great deal about himself: a very gentle boy, very patient, very outgoing. And so whenever I hear the word 'Mark' now I immediately think of the boy who liked to catch frogs. Somehow I've come in contact with him.

Sadly we are often afraid to let others get to know us at a deep level; we fence around talking about the weather, good places for holidays, the cost of living, when it would be much more revealing, but also much more terrifying, if we asked each other when we last wept and why; or if we shared what we think about as we walk around. That would be very revealing. We need to say to someone, 'Tell me who you are. What do you think and dream about? Tell me about the real you.' We should be grateful when such opportunities do arise for they are moments of grace and they draw us closer to one another. They also draw us

closer to God, for what manner of being must
he be who made so many of us, each different,
each unique?

So, we begin to meet God in a variety of
ways and we start to weave our understanding
of him through many, many impressions. But
if I am to avoid ending up with my own idea of
God, I must bring all these strands and thoughts
together and hold them up beside what God
has actually said about himself. Just as I cannot
come to a deep knowledge of another person
merely by watching them, I have one day to let
them speak to me, so it is with God – I must
let him tell me his story, I must begin to read
his word. This is where we shall need the help
of someone who is wise, not clever, someone
who has searched, listened, formed pictures and
had eventually to discard them.

What method we use for reading God's word
is up to us. Some people go systematically
through a book, while others follow the
Church's readings and thus keep in tune with
the liturgical seasons. Some use books where
texts are commented on like *Every Day With
Jesus*, written by Selwyn Hughes and published
by the Crusade for World Revival, or *The Word
Among Us* published by Turvey Abbey in
Bedfordshire. The latter publication takes the
readings from the daily liturgical celebration
of the Roman Catholic Church. Some people
prefer more detailed commentaries like those
of William Barclay. We need to find what suits

81

us. What is important is that we do not become flibbertigibbets, following no system, just going here and there.

Juan Carlos Ortiz, a Pentecostal minister from South America, said in his book *Disciple* that we ought not to underline our favourite passages in Scripture. I was surprised to read this because I had found it helpful to highlight certain passages. But the point he was making was valid – he was suggesting that we might end up only reading our favourite passages and never reading the whole word. When we begin to realise just how much God loves and cares for us, then we will be anxious to hear *all* of his word, no matter what it says to us, for we will be beginning to trust in him.

Growth

When Jesus promised to send us the Holy Spirit he said that the Spirit would 'lead' us into truth. We are not meant to get a totally passive idea that willy-nilly we will be blindly led. We have to search, look, question, agonise over – confident that all our stumblings are growth points. When God makes plants grow, he does not just give them growth, but rather he causes many complicated processes to take place within the plant and these then result in growth. So too it is with us; he uses our very activity, our searchings, even our despairs to bring us to that point where we say: 'Into your hands I commend my spirit.'

Each journey is unique. My own troubled journey brought me to the place where I had to dare to believe that the God I was hearing about was really good. This meant having to undo false impressions, and what a battle that was. It is so easy to allow bad habits of thinking to persist. Once we have begun to see that our thoughts of God are wrong, we must wage war against them, and ask God's forgiveness when we, time and time again, let falsehood lead us. Only as I began to change my internal idea of God did I find a thirst growing in me to hear what this true God had to say to me. And as I looked at words that had often frightened me, I began to see how I had misunderstood them because of the wrong image I had about the One who stood behind those words. Perhaps this is what Isaiah was talking about when he said:

> You will listen and listen again, but not
> understand, see and see again, but not
> perceive.
> For the heart of this nation has grown
> coarse,
> their ears are dull of hearing, and they have
> shut their eyes,
> for fear they should see with their eyes,
> hear with their ears,
> understand with their heart,

83

and be converted and be healed by me.
(quoted Matt. 13:14–15)

How important it is to make sure that our idea of God does resemble in some way the picture he has given us of himself. In this image of God, evil must not have its place. We must constantly revamp our ideas, knowing that no picture can capture him. Today we are learning how harmful certain foods can be; they may look attractive, even taste good, but in time their true value shows. It is the same with what we let into our minds. If I allow myself to have false ideas about God, then I will grow suspicious of him and begin to mistrust his promises. Satan could not be more delighted with such a disaster.

This is why we must seek to know God fully. We must search for him in the world around us, the world within us and in our fellow human beings. But also we must listen to what this God has told us, because what he has shared with us could never have been dreamed up by one of us; it is too magnificent, too marvellous. Our knowledge of God's word must go further than quoting: 'Thou shalt not . . .' We need to hear what this our God has done for us and we need the courage to dare to believe what he has done, what he has most surely done.

That is why there is a battle for our mind, for if we can be persuaded not to believe, then the new life won for us with such sweat and

84

pain will never come to flower, and our lives, even though they may be respectable and decent, will not be powerful and earth-shaking; they will just be nice, and we are called to be more than that.

6

Prayer: A Calling to Mind

Hear, O Israel: the Lord our God is one Lord; and you shall love the Lord your God with all your heart, and with all your soul, and with all your might. And these words which I command you this day shall be upon your heart; you shall teach them diligently to your children, and you shall talk of them when you sit in your house, and when you walk by the way, and when you lie down and when you rise. (Deut. 6:4–7) (Roman Missal)

If you want to get a sun-tan, you have to get into the sunshine. Getting into the sunshine may be very costly, it may require a lot of organisation and effort, it may entail overcoming many problems. However, the cost, the efforts and the overcoming of problems do not tan you; they only get you into the place where the sun can tan you. If you want to be holy, then you have to get into the place where God can make you holy. The place where God can make you holy is the place of faith; the place where we acknowledge and accept what God has done for us through the death and resurrection of his Son. Getting into that place requires much discipline, much hard work and there will be many difficulties to be surmounted; but the discipline, the hard work and the surmounting of the problems do not make you holy, they only get you into the place where God can work on you.

While the above analogy is helpful, the parallels break down in the last part. Sunbathing is a very passive occupation. All you have to do is sit or lie in the sun, and the sun does all the work. On the other hand standing in the place of faith requires constant acknowledging, constant accepting of God's truth. God's truth is not true because we feel it to be so, nor does it always appeal to our reason. It is true because God says it is. To keep standing in this truth involves much effort and discipline. Faith is action, it is not passive mental acceptance. The way we live changes because of what we believe. For me, prayer is standing in that place of faith.

Prayer is a subject that is vast and wide, and many people have written about it. The number of books on prayer is astounding, and in this chapter I am not really seeking to add to this enormous library. I want to say what I have found helpful. I think it is important to pray in the way you find *you* can pray. Do not go adopting other people's methods for the sake of it. If it is helpful, fine, use it and do not be afraid to adapt it. If it is not helpful, then drop it. Prayer is very personal for it is a relating to God. We all relate in our own unique way and that is why I say: pray as *you* can.

Many of us learnt of prayer as petition. 'If you want something, well, ask God for it.' Certainly prayer includes petitions, but they are only part of it. Imagine a relationship that only knew petition! 'Get me this. Come here. Find that. Put this there.' I do not think it would last very long. Relationships require sharings, tellings, listenings, ponderings, and sometimes just being together.

I do not know when I began to think of prayer as a dialogue and not as a monologue. I suppose the monologue idea stemmed from imagining that God does not speak to us. It is the word 'speak' that puts most people off. It sounds too personal, too direct. Yet Jesus said: 'I will send my Spirit to you and he will lead you into the complete truth' (John 16:8–13) – that is pretty personal and direct. In the first book of Samuel (3:1–9) we are told how the boy Samuel thought he heard the high priest Eli calling him. Three times he went to Eli, and three times Eli told him that he had not called him. The last time Eli said this to Samuel he added: 'If you hear that voice again, say: "Speak, Lord, your servant is listening".' This, I think, is a good recipe for prayer. Listen for the Lord, and then respond to him. Alas, so often our prayer is: 'Listen, Lord, for your servant is speaking.' In the last chapter we looked at the various ways that God speaks to us.

So, for me, prayer is going very deliberately into that place of faith where I take what God has said and I respond to it. That is why it is important during the day to have our antennae out, ready to catch God's messages in whatever way they come. We need to remember them. Sometimes just jotting down a phrase on a bit of paper is enough to trigger off the memory as we come into that place of faith.

I think it is important to hear God in all the ways he communicates with us. If I only listen to the God of creation, discovering his might, his power, his beauty, I will miss his work of redemption. There is so much more to God than his role as creator, great and marvellous as that is. God is in the cities and in the slums, but not all of us can readily have the privilege of seeing him in nature. Besides, there is a natural search for transcendence in all of us, and we could so easily end up by feeding on vague, misty sentiments, deluding ourselves that we are mystics. Prayer is very *practical*. It is not waltzing in the clouds. To know someone we need to know the whole of them. If we just know what they do, and have never heard them speak, then we do not know them. The same is true when I just know what someone says, and yet have never seen them do anything. I meet people who know God as creator, but do

not seem to know him as redeemer. I also meet
people who know the redeeming God, but do
not seem to know him as the creator God. I
find great richness in true ecumenical discus-
sions, for we all look at the same God in slightly
different ways.

So, quite simply, when I pray I deliberately
call to mind what God may have said in a whole
variety of ways and respond to it. When I am
deaf to his messages, then I have nothing to
respond to, and prayer becomes dry and heavy.

We can learn a great deal by looking at the
way the Church prays. She is always responding
to God's love and mercy. Take, for example,
the hymn from Morning Prayer for Sunday of
the first week in the Roman breviary:

Transcendent God in whom we live
The resurrection and the Light,
We sing to you a morning hymn
To end the silence of the night.

When early cock begins to crow
and everything from sleep awakes,
New life and hope spring up again
While out of darkness colour breaks.

Creator of all things that are,,
The measure and the end of all,
Forgiving God forget our sins,
And hear our prayer before we call.

Praise Father, Son and Holy Ghost,
Blest Trinity and source of grace,

Who calls us out of nothingness
To find in you our resting-place.

'While out of darkness colour breaks' – what a beautiful way of describing the dawn! The Church makes much use of the psalms for her prayers. In Psalm 136 there is the constant refrain: 'His steadfast love endures for ever.' While the singer of the psalm declares that God is good, God is supreme, God is Lord, this refrain keeps on being repeated. Adding our own appreciation of God to the list from the psalm, we can learn how to pray.

Meditation and contemplation

Before looking at the practical way that I try to put myself into that place of faith and respond, I would like to say something about meditation and contemplation. Modern man is distracted and scattered. So many demands are made on us that we become over-stimulated. We are called this way and that; we become divided in ourselves, bombarded by music, lights, smells. Countless things are vying for our attention. It is not surprising that when we settle down to pray, we find ourselves full of competing thoughts. Our mind is in a whirl, and it is nearly impossible to be still. We could try and conquer this problem by spending all our prayer time in 'said' prayer. At least we would feel that we are filling the time with prayer. But 'said' prayers can often just be that – said and not prayed. More importantly we then give no time to listening.

Today I meet many people from different Christian backgrounds, and they are searching for new ways to pray, for deeper ways to encounter God. How wonderful it is that we are all beginning to seek the riches in the different denominations. There seems to be a thirst to know something about the prayer of quiet. Many have tried to be still, to concentrate their thoughts on one subject, but have found their minds just too active, and so they have wrongly thought that this sort of prayer is only for certain people. Everyone, I believe, should be able to experience something of the prayer of quiet. I admit this field is a little confusing, because the words 'meditate' and 'contemplate' are used differently by different people. So a brief word to help clarify them.

Strictly speaking 'meditation' is a purely human technique. It can be used to help a person pray, but in itself it is not prayer. Because we live such scattered lives, we are often unaware of how unaware we are. Meditation is a skill to help us become aware, especially of the present moment. It is useful for all sorts of reasons, and some business firms even look for 'meditators' because they are more alert. Meditation can also help us pray. For example, most of us are quite oblivious to the various parts of our bodies; that is why meditating exercises make us concentrate on one part of our body to make us aware of our unawareness. Unconsciously we breathe. When we start thinking about this we notice that we can control our breathing, we can do it quickly or deeply, we can even stop doing it for a short time, but normally we just breathe. Most of us are unconscious of our feet, unless they are hurting, or of our back, our neck. We are also unconscious of the sounds around us, the colours, the light. Meditating makes us more fully alive to the present moment. It is a gathering of our scattered self into one. It only becomes prayer when I begin to ask: 'Who makes me breathe? Who invented sound, colour? What is he saying to me through all these things? Who gave me the various parts to my body?' It is a seeing of God here and now, not lost in some far distant history, and we respond to his touch with love and gratitude.

In this place of quiet we are better disposed to hear the God who is forever approaching us. Because my being is not stirred and filled up with many things, I can more easily recognise him. How wonderful it is to realise that my life is something that I receive minute by minute. Naturally I must take care of it, but it is not mine in the sense that I make it. Seeing life as a gift can alter the way we live, and how lovely it is to meet grateful people. Such awareness can help us to carry God into every experience of life, and this makes us more and more conscious of him speaking to us in the ordinary things. In this way we can begin to replace our wrong ideas of God with truer ones. It may have to be done painstakingly at first, but slowly the lies will give way to the truth. Scripture tells us to 'pray without ceasing' (1 Thess. 5:17). Prayer means relating and when we relate with God at every moment of the day, we are praying without ceasing.

When talking about the purely Christian variety, meditation tends to refer to when we actively engage ourselves in picturing and pondering a gospel scene, even imagining ourselves present, so as to enter more fully into the teachings. Contemplation, on the other hand, is more passive, the activity being God's rather than our own.

Unfortunately there is an aura attached to contemplative prayer. Many think it is only for special people, and they fight shy of it, and thus close themselves off to God's gift. Others, thinking it is a higher form of prayer, are anxious to be in 'club class', and they can get lost in all sorts of 'mystic' experiences which are more of the flesh than of the spirit. No idea we have of God *is* God. When we begin to realise that, we cease trying to picture him. We begin to rest in his presence. We are not too bothered how he is present, we just know he is. We cannot force this to happen in ourselves. It comes from the heart, not from our decision. It is abandoning ourselves to a God whom we really do not know, but it is done with utmost trust; and it is this abandoning that I would call contemplative prayer. Getting to be in relationship with God in this way is to set out on a journey, an exploration, a great search. The quest never finishes, you never arrive. Fr Cyprian Smith OSB, who wrote *The Way of Paradox*, said once in a talk: 'There are no gurus, no experts, we are all still searching. All we can do is share our travel notes.'

It is beyond the scope of this book to enter deeply into the field of meditation and contemplation. There are many books on the whole area, but before you plunge into reading widely you ought to find out something about the standpoint an author is writing from, perhaps by asking the advice of a friend. I know of some Christians who went to join a 'meditation group' and discovered it had little to do with what they understood meditation to be.

My own experience of prayer

Prayer has, for most people, a certain fascination. We love to read about it, we love to talk about it, but often this can be a stalling, a putting off getting down to actual prayer. What other people write about prayer seems enticing and we would like to experience the same. But often our experience is not like that and we tend to give up, or go and buy more books on prayer, and again fail to get down to it. I want now to speak about the practical steps I take in trying to pray. Remember: pray as *you* can, do not adopt what is not helpful to you.

Being a monk I am lucky, for built into our life there are times for prayer. Besides the office, which we say in common, we must all have our time for personal prayer with the Lord. Because my life is fairly regular, it is easy to find a fixed time for quiet prayer. For most people this is difficult. We live in a very hectic world and I know just how busy many of my friends are. But I think we have to be very firm about this. When there is something that we really want to do, we can usually make time for it. After all who gave us time? Surely it is right that we find some to be with God. A fixed time is helpful; if we leave it to chance, we will discover that prayer gets crowded out.

It is also good to have a place where you pray. Again we monks are spoilt. Finding a place in a house where there are small children can really be a problem. But I see married couples achieving this, the husband taking on the chores while the wife escapes for a time, and then the wife letting the husband go off before the Lord.

When I began to take prayer more seriously, that is, to say more than morning and night prayers, I did not really know what to do. I used to try to think about God and say something to him. This was not easy because being unable to visualise him I found I could not keep my attention on him. After a while I used to focus on Jesus because I could at least have some picture of him. When I was in a religious mood, this worked reasonably well, but I was not often in such a mood. Also once I had got my mind on to Jesus, I had the problem of not knowing what to say. I could not have an ordinary conversation, because he knew everything already, so it became rather natural to ask my requests. I read, and heard about, people being silent in prayer, but I discovered that I could not handle silences. Either I was soon off down some alley of distraction or I fell asleep. I tried visualising scenes from the Gospels, but I could never get much from that. I certainly never expected to hear God speak, though I think after reading some book that I did hope for a while. I tried listening but most times I heard absolutely nothing, or if I did think of something I was never sure if it was God or me that I was hearing. I came to the conclusion that God only spoke to his saints and so I gave up listening.

A time came when, through my ecumenical activities, I began to meet people who often said, 'God told me' or 'I really didn't know what to do, so I prayed and then I just knew'. I was highly suspicious and thoroughly put off. It was not my experience, but since some of the people who said this were men and women I really respected, I began to pursue this idea of God speaking. Thank God for good, wise

friends who told me to read Scriptures and start
listening to what God *has* said, before straining
to hear what he *is saying*. This was not a very
great success because the image I already had
of God prevented me from really hearing the
good news. Every time Jesus said some hard
saying, I felt guilty; and somehow when he said
a merciful thing, I could not apply it to myself.
Again it was good friends who made me take
authority over this situation. They taught me
to discipline my thoughts. They showed me how
I was living on my feelings and not on the truth.
Scripture was true, whether I felt it to be so or
not. I was not even asked to understand why,
I was simply asked to accept the word of God
as the truth. So I began taking central parts of
the gospel, and I stated them to myself imagining that God was saying this or that truth to
me. I then began to thank him for it and
to praise him and bless him. It was by no
means easy, but in some way I felt I knew what
I should do even though I found it hard. I
started to see how important it is to be on
the look-out for phrases in Scripture or moments of insight during the day, and to trea-
sure these and bring them to mind when I pray.
Since God is always communicating with us, I
will hear him if I am alert; but if I have not
looked for him, I will have missed him. I am
reminded of T. S. Eliot's poem 'Little Gidding'
(my italics):

At the source of the longest river
The voice of the hidden waterfall
And the children in the apple-tree
Not known, because not looked for
But heard, half-heard, in the stillness
Between two waves of the sea.

How important it is to be awake to the present moment.

I try to make this calling to mind of some basic truth a very real act. It is so easy to go through motions. When the psalmist tells us to 'sing a new song', I do not think it means we are to find a brand new song; rather we are to sing something we know but do it as though we have never sung it before. I find, as time goes on, that even though I am recalling a well-known truth, it often comes to mind as though it was new. If I am alone, I will speak out my gratitude and praise. I do not try to work up my feelings. I simply thank God for what he has done. Some days it is easier than others, but on the hard days I have a sense that what I am about is the most important thing I can do. When we praise God, we put him in the centre, and that is a healthy thing to do. It is hard because we like to be in the centre, that is why praise is so difficult. It truly is a sacrifice. The truths that I praise God for have, over the months, become very real. I seem to have grown in understanding of their spiritual content. For me now, the death and resurrec-

99

tion of Jesus Christ are things of central importance. I had always been told they were
important and I had accepted that, but now I
know for myself how vital they are. I think
this has come about because I have spent time
thanking God for his Son's death and resurrection even though I did not view them as top
truths.

I am beginning to see a difference between
understanding a truth because I have worked
at it with my mind, and suddenly grasping the
meaning of something when there has been no
real work on my part. When I use my mind I
get to an answer through a logical process, but
when I have a flash of enlightenment I just
know and I am not too certain why I know. In
the Roman Missal in the preface for the first
week of Lent, there is this beautiful statement:
'Whenever we call to mind the great events that
gave us new life in Christ, You (Father) bring
the image of Your Son to perfection within us.'
In other words, when we bless God for the
work he has done through his Son, we are transformed into Christ and begin to know spiritual
truths with a new mind.

It is difficult to explain exactly what happens
during my prayer time because it is a very personal time. If I sink into mooning, then I have
to stir myself and get to work. Sometimes I ask
God questions, and I am now beginning to be
confident that he will answer although maybe
not immediately. Very often I wait months

before I get some light. Some days ideas flow quite well, and in order not to lose them, I always have a notebook at hand to jot down, very briefly, what was helpful. It is interesting reading over those jottings after a month or so and seeing how themes develop.

My biggest temptation is to get excited about insights and just go over them again and again in my mind. I fear I am often delighting more in the fact that I have had an insight than in what I have seen. We can get chuffed with ourselves, and fail to notice the goodness of God in revealing something to us. When I discover this I simply ask God's forgiveness and try to turn my failure to God's profit by being amazed that he still bothers with me.

Another temptation is to cut the time short; this usually happens on the days when I am trying deliberately to praise God. I can get consumed with a desire to be up and doing something. On those days, time drags and five minutes can seem like half an hour. It is humiliating to realise that at such times I am really saying to God: 'I find you dull, and I would much prefer to be about my own business.' I know that sentiment is not really true – it is more of a feeling than a reality – but even so I ask God's forgiveness for it and beg him to change it for I cannot do so myself.

Some days I am quite vocal, putting my praise into words; other days I am silent. Not silent with emptiness, silent because I cannot find words. The more I pray, the more I become aware of my sinfulness – not so much sinful actions, though of course those still persist, but rather an understanding of how self-centred I still am in spite of God's graces. All these discoveries do not flatter us, but then we do not pray to have ourselves flattered. I suppose it stands to reason that the nearer we approach God, the more we are going to notice the blemishes in ourselves. God does not reveal these to humiliate us; he does it so that we will honestly confess them and then experience the truth that his Son has borne them for us.

In prayer we undertake a vast journey from self to God. It is a journey that we cannot accomplish by our own efforts. We may start praying for very selfish motives, we may be looking for consolations, the satisfaction of being thought holy, an insurance policy for a happy hereafter – God in his mercy is very patient. He spoils us with consolations and joy. In time, though, he begins to prune, and prayer becomes dull and heavy. Alas, most give up at this moment. It really is a moment for growth. And so we need to know about the seasons of prayer, the good times and the difficult.

Dryness in prayer

When we notice that our prayer has dried up, become routine and dull, our first reaction ought to be to look at our lives. Has something gone wrong, a bad relationship grown up, or is there some unrepented fault? All these things can cause a clouding in our prayer life. Care must be taken that as we examine ourselves we do not become over-scrupulous, for none of us is perfect. What we are looking for is some new and recent fault. When nothing obvious can be found, and if the dryness continues, then it may be that God is purifying us. The trouble is that if prayer is always found to be rewarding, then, we could so easily do it just for that. So, God may have to dry things up a bit, to make us ask the question: 'Am I here for me or for him?'

There are both little nights, which are quickly over, and winter seasons, which can endure for very long periods. During these periods we need a wise companion, and they are not always easily found. This experience of a long, dry patch can be extremely painful, and there seems to be no good got from it. It is one thing to pray to a God who does not appear to be listening, but it is quite something else to pray to a God whom you no longer think exists. I know when I went through a very lengthy dry period, it seemed impossible to convey to anyone the agony I experienced. The people I found the most helpful were those who just stood with me in my doubts and did not argue. No number of doubts add up to an unbelief. It is not wrong to doubt, question, ponder – all that is part of the journey of faith, but there is a terrible loneliness when one stands in a place where others never seem to pass.

When prayer is dry, that is the time when methods, plans, schemes can be useful. Words taken from a familiar prayer, for example the Lord's Prayer, can be thoughtfully gone through. Do not judge your prayer by what you get out of it, rather look at how much you put into it. The very fact that you give time, you stay there, even though you are empty, is a good sign. Imagine visiting a sick person only because you enjoyed it.

Prayer is this vast journey from where self is centre to where God is centre. Such a journey is bound to be painful. We can deceive ourselves and imagine that we have put God in the centre, when all the time we are admiring ourselves for putting God in the centre. When prayer is empty, and yet we still continue with it, then at least we are beginning not to be there for our own comfort. These barren periods are necessary and God knows when best to send them. They prove to be great growth points.

7

A Sure Foundation: Concluding Thoughts

Therefore, everyone who listens to these words of mine and acts on them will be like a sensible man who built his house on rock. Rain came down, floods rose, gales blew and hurled themselves against that house, and it did not fall: it was founded on rock. (Matt. 7:25)

Living in the Spirit is not to live by holy nudges. God certainly can and does nudge us, but from the way some people talk you would imagine that the Holy Spirit sits on their shoulders directing their every move. That God could do this, I have no doubt; but that God would do this, I doubt very much, save on rare occasions.

To live by the Spirit is first to know what the Spirit came to reveal. Secondly, it is to believe what the Spirit reveals. Thirdly, it is to keep in mind what the Spirit reveals. One of the main problems facing the Church is, I think, the ignorance that so many Christians have about the central message of the gospel. The gospel covers many important topics, and different ones can be adopted by different people as their favourite; in doing this it is so easy for the main message to get marginalised and for it to lose its significance as a life-giving truth. The central point of the gospel is that Jesus died for our sins and rose to new life. In dying he paid the consequences for our sins, and because, as God, any action of his had infinite value, the result of sin, a blockage between humanity and God, has been removed. This means that it is possible for people to be in relationship again with God; but each individual has to accept what God has done, and how God has done it. Senior citizens now have all sorts of benefits available to them, but they have to prove that they are senior citizens; so, too, we have to prove we are eligible to receive what Christ has done for us, and we do that by submitting our sins, and confessing that Jesus, through his death, has paid for those sins.

That is not all: there is more to this basic truth. Death could not keep hold of Jesus, the innocent man, and on his resurrection, he became the new man. Here was someone over whom evil had no power. This work of Jesus was not just to remove the barrier caused by sin, it was to take away the very sinfulness of man by giving him a new life. Life is not just something we have, like a suitcase, which we keep in the attic and use from time to time; no, it is something that we must always use. We live life, we do not just have it. So, too, with this new life; it is not just something we have, it is something we need constantly to use. In order to do this, we daily, hourly have to remind ourselves that, with Christ, we are dead in our old life and are alive with his new life. It is this conscious, daily decision to live in that place of faith, that enables us to know the power of the risen Lord. Every thought or anxiety that threatens to cast us into gloom or insecurity must be firmly grasped and expelled. As we find again and again that place of peace, we will experience the truth of the words: 'I am the Way . . . no one can come to the Father save through me' (John 14:6). It is not that all problems will fade away, we may well have to go right through the centre of the storm, but there comes an inner certainty that we cannot be snatched out of the hand of God.

The difficulty that I meet as I try to counsel and help people stems from their distorted idea of God and his word. Having suffered from this myself, I know how effective it can be in numbing the power of the gospel to set one free. Imagine what it feels like to be told that Christianity is the answer to the mystery of life, and yet not experience that as true! It puts you in a terrible spot. You are told 'this is the truth', and because you do not experience it as true, you feel guilty, isolated, alone. You may not have the guts to abandon it completely, after all there are some terrible threats attached to leaving, and so you settle for being a misfit, and you cover up, putting a good face on it all.

I really understand the bitterness and resentments that some Christians carry around buried deep within their being. All these hurts can have different effects – some people become belligerent and hostile, others turn in on themselves and end up insecure, fearful, over-submissive, full of self-reproach.

In this book I have tried to make you look at who God is for you. It is so easy to answer the party line and deceive ourselves. For years I would never admit my inmost feelings about God, not so much because I was ashamed of them, but because I did not really know they were there. These inmost thoughts need exposing to the light; we must hold them up to God's own revelation of himself and be honest about what we see. As I have said before, we would be greatly helped by having some wise, not clever, person to be a sounding board.

I have also tried to spell out the wound that is in us and to look at what God has told us about its origin. This, I know, is walking into a thorny area, which could easily deflect us from trying to hear what God is saying. I suppose it is not surprising that we should find such difficulty in accepting responsibility for something which we did not actually do. If we are honest we will find an inner resentment, but that reaction is the very symptom of what has gone wrong. We are looking at things from our point of view and not from God's. If you have a camera with the viewfinder out of line with the lens, although you may focus your viewfinder on what you wish to photograph, in fact your lens is focused on something else. We were made for God, and we centre on self, and what is worse when we think we are centering on God, often we are fixed on ourselves. Because of the wound deep within us, we find it very difficult to look at things save from our own point of view. We much prefer to argue our case, and thus put off that moment of confessing.

We have the same trouble over the salvation won for us by Jesus Christ. It is very difficult to be on the receiving end. Our whole western education teaches us to be self-sufficient, and so it is very natural that we should take that over into religion – we want some credit for being saved. We can argue that it has been no easy task to remain faithful, we may list the sacrifices, tot up the cost, but the fact remains that you cannot win eternal life. Eternal life is God-life. There is nothing a creature could do to merit God-life. A good ape could never merit human life. Besides Jesus never said that following him would be easy. Our self-loving being will resist all the way while God works his transformation in us. We will certainly be rewarded in heaven for the good we do, but good works cannot merit eternal life, which we need for entering heaven in the first place.

To be hazy about these central truths is to cut at the very heart of the gospel. Anything that can divert us from life-giving truth and make us occupied with some other truth, even though important, can successfully keep us from the power of the gospel. What is worse, we can stay within the ranks of the Church, and yet somehow never be fully Church, because to be ignorant about what God has done for us in Christ Jesus virtually means that we do not have faith in his saving work. It is faith in that truth that gives life.

Ignorance about what God has done is serious, but it is not enough to know what he has done, we need to believe it. Here again we can mistake intellectual assent for faith. Faith has to be demonstrated in action, and by action I do not just mean good works. I mean living my daily life according to what I profess to believe. If I live full of fear of God, anxious with regard to my salvation, I am demonstrating that I do not trust in the saving work of Jesus Christ and still basically rely on my own performance. I do believe also that as we allow the new life of Christ to develop in us, we will do the good deeds that have been commanded us: 'We are God's work of art, created in Christ Jesus to live the good life as from the beginning he meant us to live it' (Ephesians 2:10). The sad thing is that we can set out to do great good but in our own power: 'it is the spirit that gives life, the flesh has nothing to offer' (John 6:63). If we boast that we have the life of Christ in us and yet never

110

give any indication by our action that this is so, then the absence of fruit makes others question the truth of what we say. Our belief is betrayed by our actions.

We are asked to believe that through the death and rising of Jesus our sins have been dealt with and that we have received a new life to enable us to live in a new way. Once upon a time that truth, though never actually denied, was not central in my life. Christianity for me was behaving in a morally acceptable way. It was up to me to get my life into shape. I became what I now call a 'muscular Christian'. I gritted my teeth and did my best. Results followed: I learnt to smile when I was angry, I could keep a reasonable exterior calm when I was impatient. But that was the trouble – it was only external. Later when I began to learn the truth about Christ's death and resurrection, I did not find that I applied what I knew to my living. I remained the muscular monk. For a long time I was not conscious of this dichotomy; but as I began to be aware of it, I was puzzled as to how to apply the truth that through the cross of Jesus I was saved. Did this mean I just waited until the power of God set me free? Just what was I meant to do? I think this is a good example of how our darkened mind works. I was suffering from a spiritual blindness – it all seemed nonsense to me, although I knew deep down that it was not right to just sit around until the saving power came upon me. I had to

111

do something, but that something was not to continue with my muscular efforts.

In time I began to see that my efforts were to be channelled into fervent acts of faith in the cross of Jesus. I had to praise God deliberately for what he had achieved through Christ. The change was not sudden, but gradually I began to see that habits which had held me in their grip did not seem to be so dominant. While I was spending this time praising and thanking God, I did of course do my best to control my life – but I now knew these efforts of mine were not the solution. They, in a sense, were the best I could do, until the Lord had mercy on me and made his Son's work effective in me. Remember the example I gave about rowing or sailing a boat. When you row a boat, it is your effort that moves it; when you sail a boat, it is the wind that moves it, but you have a lot to do. You do not just sit there, you cooperate with the power of the wind.

To believe is to act out the truth that you know. The devil knows the truth, but it has not helped him because he refuses to accept it. To be able continually to act out this truth we must constantly call it to mind. Because of the way we have been brought up, because of what we have learnt or picked up unconsciously from life, our ways of thinking need changing. We have fallen into patterns of thought that come from the world and not from the Spirit. Someone said that religion is not taught, it is caught. There is some truth in that, for gospel truths can be passed on to us and they come to be part of what we know, but do not become a life-giving experience. There is all the difference in the world between knowing about someone – I can be taught that – and knowing someone, which only happens through direct contact. It is the Holy Spirit who provides us with that direct contact. Scripture, without the aid of the Spirit, can fail to introduce us to the real Jesus. I have met too many people who even after honest searching in Scripture have failed to meet the true Christ. They have confessed to me that the Jesus they met they did not find warm and approachable. I am convinced that they were bringing into their thinking some very early impression that they had of him. He was for them, and alas for so many, the pale Galilean who was very correct and always right, but rather forbidding. I can remember reading on a church hall board a sign which said, 'God is watching'.

Hence our patterns of thought need careful examination – are we allowing wrong and false pictures to colour our thinking, thus affecting our every encounter with Christ? To be able to control this habit, we need to spend time consciously and deliberately calling to mind the great events that gave us new life in Christ, and then praising and thanking God for his great love and mercy. This is not magic, it is not a matter of just saying formulas of belief; what is

113

required is a deep, convinced faith. Faith is a gift, and we must continually ask for it and exercise it. This exercise is what I call prayer: a deliberate responding to God's revelation. In prayer we remind ourselves of God's plan and check how much we live by that. We must not be like the man in the Letter of James (1:22–5) who looked into the mirror and then went away and forgot what he had seen. There are powerful forces working to make us forget the central message.

I see prayer as the continual dialogue in which God reminds us of all he has done, and we, in accepting and consenting to this, experience its power to change our lives. Quite simply we need to know what God has done for us, believe in its efficacy and continually keep it in mind as we walk through life. As we obey God's word already spoken, we will begin to realise it is actually being spoken to us, and thus we will be open to hear the God who does speak to us his personal word.

Jesus was also led by the Holy Spirit

Jesus, himself, was led by the Spirit and at first there must have been a growing excitement in him as he saw more clearly his role and his Father backing his words with signs and wonders. This enthusiasm would have been caught by his own disciples and by the crowds as they saw that Jesus fitted their picture of the

114

expected Messiah. 'Here is the one who was promised. With such power and miracles, he will surely deliver us from all our foes' – these and similar words would have spread like wildfire among the people.

But a time came when Jesus changed. He became more mysterious. Even before the transfiguration, he began to hint that he was to die. After the experience on the mountain, he set his face towards Jerusalem and seemed determined to go there even though he foretold that he would be arrested and killed. What happened on that mountain? Did Moses and Elijah speak with him about his passing? The face of Jesus shone, not as though a light was shining on him, but as though a light was shining out from him. Was he receiving an inner illumination about the Father's will for him? Was he seeing clearly what the Father was asking? This would account for his changed attitude after the vision and why he began instructing his disciples about his passing: 'He was telling them, "The Son of Man will be delivered into the hands of men; they will put him to death; and three days after he has been put to death he will rise again". But they did not understand what he said and were afraid to ask him' (Mark 9:31–2). I am not saying that Jesus did not know until then what he was destined for. Before the transfiguration he had rounded on Peter when he tried to turn him away from his foretold death. We read in Scripture that Jesus grew in wisdom and knowledge, and I feel that on the mountain he gained clarification about his future, and thus on coming down he determined to go to Jerusalem and the mode of his life changed.

I am forever speculating about how much Jesus knew. As God, of course, he would know everything. Did that knowledge affect his human knowledge? I have no idea; that is the sort of question theologians like to grapple with. I tend to side with those who say that his human knowledge was incomplete. I find comfort in thinking of him also in the dark, following blindly the Father's will. What was asked of him was so opposite to fulfilling the role of liberator. He was asked to fail, to be conquered, to be hounded out of the city and to die as a criminal. Could he see through all that to the victory to follow? It is difficult to tell. I find it good to wrestle with such questions, and in prayer to ask the Lord to enlighten me. The point I want to make here is what happened to the Master will surely happen to the disciple; we, too, will suffer hardship, and perhaps for no apparent reason.

Teilhard de Chardin in *Le Milieu Divin* talks of a time of positive growth and development, and he sees that as an essential part of one's life; but he also talks of a time of diminishment, and this for the sake of being in another. I regret that the gospel came to me first as diminishment. I heard about giving up, renouncing, dying, before I had heard, 'Be fruitful, multiply, fill the earth and conquer it' (Genesis 1:28). God certainly does prune, but if there has been no growth, how can he prune? Also if I do not experience the hand that prunes as first loving and tender, then how can I trust when the time for cutting back arrives? Jesus had perfect confidence in his Father. He who loved the lilies of the field and talked about such homely things as harvest, grape growing, fishing, must have delighted in this world and forever have seen traces of his Father. Thus when the Father revealed his deep plan, Jesus was anxious to fulfil it no matter how strange it may have appeared.

'I will send my Spirit to you and he will lead you into the complete truth' (John 16:13). That promise is made to every one of us, and we need to allow the Spirit to challenge us over our ideas of God; we must be forever growing, seeing things in new and deeper ways. Not only is the Spirit in us, we also have the Lord who walked in trust of his Father living in us, and he promised:

> If anyone loves me he will keep my word,
> and my Father will love him,
> and we shall come to him
> and make our home with him. (John 14:23)

To walk in the way of the spirit, without the directing of the Holy Spirit, runs the very real risk of being led off down a labyrinth of ways, enticing, appealing, but alas a subtle self-centred search into our natural yen for mysticism. We are seeking after God, not mysticism. This quest requires discipline, determination and guidance. But when all is said and done, we find in the end that what we fondly thought was our search for God, was really his search for us and much of our striving has been our refusal to be found by him.

'Not my will, but yours' – how difficult it is to move from an attitude of heroic sacrifice to one of convinced, joyful surrender, and to discover yet again, it was not our achievement but his achieving in us.

You Will
Receive Power

Introduction

I grew up not knowing very much about the Holy
Spirit. In those days we called him Holy Ghost, and
that was not very helpful. When I became a monk
and priest much of my studies were spent consider-
ing the Father and the Son – we did not devote a
great deal of time to the Spirit in those days.

However, towards the latter part of this century,
there has been a renewed interest in the Holy Spirit,
much of it caused by the Pentecostal Movement.
This movement, which sprang from the Pentecostal
Church and entered the main-line Protestant
Churches in the 1950s and the Roman Catholic
Church in the 1960s, emphasises the power of the
Holy Spirit manifested chiefly in the charismatic gifts
or gifts of the Spirit.

I became involved in this renewal and my first
real encounter with the Holy Spirit was through the
charisms, the power gifts. Up till then much of my
understanding of the gospel message had been concentrated on dying to self, carrying one's cross, being
brave under trial. Suddenly I was discovering a
whole new side to the gospel – the Lord in rising
had conquered and we in his name were sent out to
minister his victory to the broken-hearted, the lame,

the sick. We were not called to carry every cross and offer up every trial: we were to minister the Lord's victory and set people free. It was heady stuff.

It seems amazing to me that I could have missed this side of the gospel and concentrated on the dying to self, the brave embracing of hardships; but when you do not read the whole gospel and just confine yourself to what the Sunday readings give, then I suppose it is not surprising if you end up with an impoverished understanding.

The next lesson I had to learn was not to jettison the suffering-cross side of the gospel but to learn to live in this strange land where 'all has-been-achieved' and yet somehow 'is-not-yet-achieved' in us. Both themes are in the one gospel and it is neither victory all the way nor suffering and pain all the way – strange bedfellows indeed.

When I was asked to write this book it was intended to be on the gifts of the Holy Spirit, but the more I worked on it the more I realised that that would emphasise the power side of the gospel and thus give a lopsided view of the Holy Spirit's work. He has come to do far more than just give us charismatic gifts.

I believe that there are two sorts of empowering that the Spirit does. One is personal and is concerned with making all that Jesus has achieved for us effective in us. Jesus came to put our Adam life to death and give us a share in his risen, new life. In the fourth eucharistic prayer we say: 'That we might no longer live for ourselves but for him, he sent the Holy Spirit from you, Father, as his first gift to those who believe, to complete his work on earth and bring us the fulness of grace.' This clearly expresses the

2

first work of the Holy Spirit, which empowers us to live a new life on the condition that we let go of the old. There is the rub. We have constantly to let go of the old life applying the Cross of Jesus, and to rise to new life with him. This does not just happen; our task is to allow God to make it happen, and he acts when we have faith in what Jesus has done. So this first empowering of the Spirit has much to do with sacrifice, self-surrender, and death.

The other empowering is the gifting with spiritual power gifts or charisms. These gifts are not new to the Church. They may, however, be new to us and the very existence of a renewal to restore charisms shows that these gifts are, or have been, largely unknown to the Church at large. Charisms are spiritual gifts for service belonging to the Holy Spirit and those who manifest them are merely messengers – they are given something to deliver.

With the rediscovery of the power gifts of the Spirit during this century it is very important to keep a wise and healthy balance between the two empowerings of the Holy Spirit. '... You will receive power when the Spirit comes on you, and then you will be my witnesses not only in Jerusalem but throughout Judaea and Samaria, and indeed to the ends of the earth' (Acts 1:8). That power entails both the power to die to self and the power to do wonders in the service of others.

In this book, I will begin by examining the personal empowering of the Holy Spirit to make effective in us what Christ has achieved on the cross. I will then go on to look in detail at the various charisms or spiritual gifts, attempting to show what each gift means and how we might be more open to receiving them in our lives and the life of the Church. I will end by briefly examining the thorny question of baptism in the Spirit and assessing the value of prayer meetings.

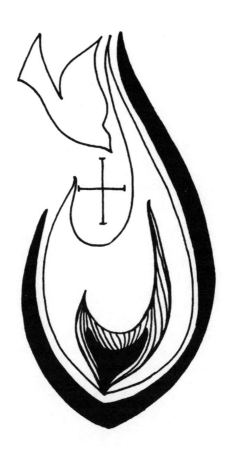

1

Holy Spirit as Guide

It is quite possible to grow up in a Christian environment and to be seen as a practising Christian attending church regularly, and yet fail to grasp the main point of the gospel. I know this is true because it happened to me.

The best teaching in the world does not guarantee that it is perfectly received. I do not actually believe that I had the best teachers possible, but that is neither here nor there, for it is what is received that matters and that may not have much to do with what is given. Much can happen to the message from the moment it leaves the teacher and the moment it arrives in the recipient.

I certainly believed that Jesus Christ was the Son of God and that he had come among us to save us; but my understanding of him as saviour was that he had come as an example to teach us how to live so that we could merit salvation. In other words everything he did or said was as an example for us. Therefore his dying was an example of how we too must obey God no matter what the cost. His rising

7

was, for me, a confirmation that he was God and therefore we had better listen to all he had taught and obey him.

These wrong ideas of mine, and how subtle the mistake was, made it perfectly possible to listen to sermons, especially moralistic ones, and yet never have my errors challenged. The more I heard about discipline, the harder I tried to live the perfect life. I admired goodness and I was encouraged to work hard at it. Reading lives of saints was a great source of inspiration and I felt a desire to imitate them. Even when I heard about Jesus dying for me, I still saw it as a heroic example and one that inspired me to greater efforts.

This way of thinking received a shattering blow when I heard the good news of the gospel being spelt out very clearly by people of the Protestant Church. Like Luther, I suddenly realised that I did not save myself, in fact I had already been saved by all that Jesus had done at Calvary. Such a revelation was devastating and it took all my courage to allow myself to listen to my new understandings and to explore them.

I think we often imagine that once we are baptised then we are evangelised; so the tendency is for the Church to teach the baptised doctrines and church practices, which I suppose is the old idea of what catechism was about. There is, I believe, a desperate need for the baptised actually to be evangelised. To evangelise means to bring someone to understand that God so loved the world that he sent his Son to take on himself our sins and suffer the consequence in our place. Evangelisation is not something that happens once. True there is a first moment when we see what the gospel means, but then it takes all our life to accept it fully and to permit it to change us completely.

In this process of acceptance and change, the Holy Spirit acts as our guide. Jesus promised to send us his Holy Spirit telling us that the Spirit would lead us into truth, teaching us and reminding us of all that Jesus had said (John 14:26; 16:13). The Holy Spirit works directly on our spirit and we come to know the truth without really being able to say how or why we know it. It is less a matter of human reasoning than of inspiration. When we read Scripture, for example, we can understand a certain amount with our minds, but in order to have a deep knowledge in our hearts we need the guidance and inspiration of the Holy Spirit.

In my own experience I think I imagined that a flood of insights would hit me if I really gave time to reading Scripture. I had been fascinated and thrilled when I had listened to some Protestant preachers expound the Bible. They seemed to have such insights and were able to draw so much from texts that had remained a closed book to me. I think I imagined that the Spirit would enable me to see all the nuances provided I gave time to the study of the Word.

The reality was different. I did not get exciting insights and good material for sermons; what I found instead was that I began to trust what the Word said. It was not clever understandings that came, rather a conviction that this was God's Word and with it came a great desire to trust the Word and to live it no matter what. I was not advancing in

9

understanding, but rather in knowing that God had spoken and it was my duty to obey.

This is how the Spirit works, less through human reasoning than through conviction and a deep moving in our hearts. Human intelligence is important, but in the realm of the Spirit it is limited; we certainly need to ponder and reflect but always remembering that firm assurance of faith is beyond the human intellect.

REFLECTIONS

● It is important to know how we really think of God. We may be able to give the right answers, such as he is loving, kind, merciful, but are they our answers? Or are we giving the responses we have learnt? We must not worry if our answers are wrong. The first step in putting them right is to know they are wrong.

● Try and be honest while you think about how you experience God. It may be helpful to write down what you feel.

● Then simply tell God how you feel, ask his forgiveness and ask the Spirit, who is in you, to lead you into the truth.

● As you read the next chapter compare your ideas about God with what God has said about himself through his Church and Scripture. Also see how much he has done for us.

2

The Good News

 The Holy Spirit is able to convict us of the truth in Scripture, but in order to understand these truths properly we need good teaching. We cannot accept the truth and obey it until we first learn it.

I have been a priest long enough to realise that there are still many who imagine heaven and eternal life are merited by being good or by performing some heroic act. When you mention heaven you will hear people say things like: 'I wonder if I will ever make it there?' Or 'If anyone deserves to get to heaven it is old Bill, why all life long he suffered.' 'If after all this trouble I do not make it to heaven, then I shall be very upset.' I know these remarks are not to be taken seriously, but they do reflect an attitude.

Or again we can see how quickly popular devotions spread. 'Say this prayer, it is never found to fail.' 'Do the first nine Fridays and you will get to heaven.' 'Or the first five Saturdays.' 'Have a blessed candle in your house for the three days of darkness that are to come.' 'Add this prayer in between the decades of the rosary.' 'Display this holy image in your house.' Why do we have this plethora of devotions? I fear it is because the good news has not been preached clearly and people are looking for security. I am not against devotions, nor private revelations, but when more trust is put in them than in what Jesus Christ has achieved through his death and resurrection, then something has gone seriously wrong.

There are thousands of things to know about Jesus and all that he said and did, but he came for one reason and one reason alone – and that was to save the world through his death and resurrection. It would be more than tragic if we knew a lot about Jesus but somehow never came to know the real reason for his coming.

God so loved this world that he sent his Son into our human family. Jesus, who is sinless, consents to become one of our family taking to himself 'a nature like man's sinful nature' (Romans 8:3–4, Roman Breviary) and willingly bearing the consequences of that.

When Adam sinned, he rejected God and thus he experienced separation from God. I think we need to get rid of the idea of God being angry and therefore rejecting us. It is we who have rejected him, and the consequences have fallen on us. There is nothing we can do to right this problem. But God wants to put it right, so he has sent his only Son to bear in himself the consequence of our sins, because he, being God, is able to live obedient to the Father even in a human nature made in the likeness of sinful flesh.

Sin is our refusal to live for God; we were not

made for ourselves, we are creatures and are made for God. Jesus, in consenting to stand where sin has put humankind, is saying on behalf of humankind: 'You, Father, are just and right and I, as one of the human family, willingly stand separated from you because I have been made sin in your sight. I obediently embrace this consequence of humanity's sin.'

Because Jesus is God any act of his has infinite value. By taking our sins on himself and willingly accepting the terrible separation from his beloved Father, he has removed the consequences of sin. Death was unable to hold onto the Holy One of God, so at the command of the Father Jesus rose thus starting a new race filled with new life. This does not mean the whole human family has now been automatically pardonned; but it does mean pardon and new life is available *to any one who accepts this saving act of Jesus*. This is what salvation by faith means. It means putting our trust in what Jesus has done for us. However, we cannot put our trust in this truth if we have not been taught it, and there are many, as I know by experience, for whom this is by no means clear.

St Paul puts it very clearly in his letter to the Colossians (1:27). Here we are told in no uncertain terms what God's plan is. 'God's plan is this: to make known his secret to his people, this rich and glorious secret which he has kept for all his people. And the secret is this: Christ is in you, which means you will share the glory of Christ.' It could hardly be put more clearly and so to put our trust in novenas, holy medals, certain prayers and not in Christ is to disobey. It is not that these things are wrong, but

15

they can never be a substitute for Christ's saving work.

Immediately, now, the question of the unbeliever rises up. How can those who have never heard of Jesus, or have never come to believe in him, go to heaven? I do believe God is a merciful God and I do not want to start judging those who have a different faith. God knows everyone's story and I cannot believe he will condemn those who through no fault of their own have never heard the good news. The question I am asking is, do we, the Christian believers, really believe that Jesus is our way? By getting involved with worrying about unbelievers, we can duck the question – do we ourselves really believe?

I think there still lingers among Catholics the idea that heaven is won as a reward for good work, and such an idea makes a lot of sense because logically you will not get to heaven by being bad. It is very difficult suddenly to switch from one way of under-standing to another. My reaction to first hearing that we did not merit heaven was one of anger. 'Why, that's not fair – it means we will all get there, the good and the bad. So what's the use of being good?' It is so hard for us to understand our alienation from God. We cling to the idea that we are able to put it all right, and so we fondly go on imagining that our being nice and decent is in some way going to appease God and win our forgiveness. It is very hard for a decent, law-abiding person to see their need of redemption. Was that why Jesus commended those who were spiritually poor? They at least knew their need of a saviour.

Good works will not merit our entry into heaven.

16

We enter heaven through accepting what Jesus has done for us by dying and rising in obedience to the Father's will. Our good works will be rewarded *in* heaven, but not *with* heaven.

REFLECTIONS

- Up until now how have you understood salvation? As a work of Christ or as something you earn? In what way do you understand Christ's passion and death? Was he giving us a heroic example of obedience or was there something more to all he did?
- Ask the Spirit to help you understand.
- Have you understood that you do not make yourself holy by doing holy things? We first need to be holy and then we can do holy things.
- Do you now see how we become holy?

3

Through Faith

 Once we have heard the truth about salvation through faith in Christ, we have conscientiously to apply it to the way we live for it is not just knowing the truth that sets us free; we also have to live it. We have to live through faith.

When our basic ideas of God and Christianity are wrong, then any subsequent idea about God will be influenced by what we already think. Our way of thinking has become a habit and we need systematically to dismantle it by replacing it with the truth. St Paul calls this 'having a new mind'. The first step along this route is to admit our basic ideas of God have been wrong, or if not wrong, far too small, and to ask his forgiveness.

Spiritual truths are not learnt quickly. It is very difficult to put our trust in what God says because often we neither feel nor are convinced that it is true. I remember once doing a six-week course with a parish group during Lent. Each week I would give them a few Scripture quotes and ask them to try and

practise living those truths during the week. At the
end of the first week, most of them confessed they
had forgotten even to read the Scripture quotes. At
the end of the second week, having remembered to
read the quotes, they forgot all about them in the
business of the day. After the third week, having
remembered the quotes, they found they seriously
doubted their truth as they tried to live them during
the day. It was only in the fourth and fifth week that
they began to put their trust in God's Word and to
ignore their feelings and the arguments that came
up as they tried to live what God said.

In the last chapter we saw what Jesus has done
for us by dying and rising. This act of his is enough
to save the whole of humanity. However, this does
not mean that we have nothing to do. All gifts need
to be *both* given *and* received. Jesus has done suf-
ficient for our salvation and if we want this to affect
us then we have to receive this gift from him.

What God is saying to us is: 'I sent my Son to take
your sins on himself and die in your place. Death is
for sinners, and since my Son was innocent, death
could not hang onto him and at my word he rose
from the dead. He has done all this for you. If you
want to benefit from this then it is up to you to
accept what he has done by putting your trust in his
sacrifice. Then your sins will be forgiven and you
will be given a new life so that you can live in a new
way.'

It is this act of faith that is required of a person
offering themselves for baptism. At the baptism of
an infant, this act of faith is made by the parents for
the child. Later that child is expected to ratify this
step by his or her own act of faith in what Jesus has

done. When this act of faith remains lacking either by the parents, or by the child who has never ratified it personally, then although the sacrament has been valid, it has not had its full effect because it has never been fully consented to. This can easily be remedied by that individual making a simple act of faith in what Jesus has done. In this way we fan into flame our baptism.

It is this act of faith that is often missing from people's lives. Frequently faith is thought of as assenting to God's existence, believing that Jesus is the Son of God, giving intellectual agreement to doctrines and doing one's best to live a decent life. There is, however, more to faith than that. Faith is putting our trust in what Jesus has done and not in our own achievements.

This vital act of faith is not a one-for-all-time assent. True, there is a moment when we begin to believe, but belief has to be an ongoing act. If we decide to sing a song, then in order for the song to continue, we have continually to decide to sing.

If we are going to change the way we live our lives we need to begin listening to what God has already said and shape our lives accordingly. This means we have deliberately to inform ourselves about what Jesus has said and done for us, and accept his way of doing things.

The Teachings of the Church

The Church teaches many things but not every truth is of the same value. We are encouraged to go on pilgrimages, to say the rosary, to fast, to intercede for the world, to give to charity – the list is endless.

There are also pious customs such as wearing blessed medals, scapulars, venerating holy pictures – but to count any of these things as of more value than what God has done for us through his Son Jesus Christ is to be in serious error. It is of paramount importance that we know the real teachings of the Church. Salvation comes through the death and resurrection of Jesus Christ. This does not mean we have to embark on an academic course, but we do need to know what God has said and done for us so as to be able to put our trust in him.

The Importance of Scripture

Scripture remained largely closed to me until I had learnt the good news that I do not save myself. I then began to see that message of salvation in all I read in Scripture, and I have become more and more convinced that it is only after we have been evangelised that our minds become open to receive this message.

One of the difficulties of grasping the message of salvation is we are told that *something has been done but we do not yet experience it as having been done*. Scripture tells me to believe that I have been saved, but I have to face the problem that I do not appear to be saved by the way I live my life. The problem is it takes time to change from trusting in what one thinks one can do to trusting in what the Lord has done for us. Imagine that you are having to study a certain subject and you feel it is far beyond you; but you have a good friend who promises to help you. That help is always available to you, but you do not benefit from it until you go and ask for it. We are called

24

upon to believe that he, who conquered the evil one, is dwelling within us ready to share his power with us. We will never benefit from this power until we draw on it. To live by faith is to live in this truth.

Knowing that Jesus Christ died on the Cross for our sins is not the same as accepting this truth as something that personally affects us. It is all too easy to say, 'Lord, by your Cross and Resurrection, you have set us free' and then live as though we become free by our will-power alone.

We need to avoid two extremes: one which says 'Alleluia. Jesus has done it all, there is nothing left to do', and the other which is the attitude, 'It is all up to me.' We must remember that those who refuse to go into the sunshine will never get a suntan. This is the heart of the gospel and from it all else springs. This is the power Paul referred to when he said, 'I am not ashamed of the good news: it is the power of God saving those who believe' (Romans 1:16).

Prayer

St Benedict began his Rule with the words: 'Listen to the words of the Master'. The word 'rule' was not a help to me when I entered the monastery, because it only confirmed the idea to me that it was all up to me. I tended to look at the Rule as instruction on how to become holy. I felt that if I did everything as the Rule said, then I would achieve sanctity.

That was to misunderstand St Benedict. It was not surprising that I should do this since I had mis-understood the gospel, and this again confirms to me that we must never assume other people have been evangelised. They may appear very zealous and keen, but that could all be the result of being misled.

St Benedict was saying that if you spend time listening to Scripture, listening to the fathers, and to your superiors, then, if you have really listened (and how hard that is), you will have heard what God has done for you. Then you will begin to understand that it is not up to you to achieve but to allow God to achieve Christ's work in you.

Obviously if we are to listen to God, the fathers and our teachers, some discipline will be required on our part, but after we begin to hear God's loving plan, 'our hearts shall be enlarged, and we shall run with unspeakable sweetness of love in the way of God's commandments. . .' (Prologue: Rule of St Benedict).

Prayer is a dialogue, preferably with God speaking first. It is only by listening to God that we will begin to hear what he has already done and we will ask with fervour that his will be done.

Having listened to God, and that means having allowed God's ideas really to enter our minds and not to have gone dancing off with some idea that was our own, he now waits to hear our response. When the Church prays she puts before us what God has done and then she puts words of adoration, worship and thanksgiving into our mouths. The more we allow the Spirit of God to enlighten us with God's plans, the more we will want to express our love and thanksgiving. I am not talking about an emotion here. No matter what we may feel like God has done great things for us and he is worthy always of our thanks. Praising and blessing God is an act of faith, and as we have seen, faith saves us. So we need to spend time in prayer to God and much of that prayer will be a response in gratitude to God for what he has done.

Action

We need to do more, though, than read, study and pray. All this must bear fruit in action. As we acquire new minds so our actions ought to change. Actions that do not spring from the power of the One who dwells within us, remain just human actions and will be either laboured or cold. As we begin to allow the divine nature to possess us, then our actions become his. There is a difference between doing charitable acts and being charitable. I used to imagine that if I did kind things then I would become kind. I now realise it is the other way round, I have to be kind to do genuinely kind acts to others. If I am to be kind then I need a total transformation, something impossible for me but more than possible for God. Jesus tells us to love one another as he loves us – an impossible action unless he himself loves others through us. We are not called to imitate Christ, but to be one with him.

For this to happen we have much to do. Paul tells us to 'give up your old way of life; you must put aside your old self, which gets corrupted by following illusory desires. Your mind must be renewed by a spiritual revolution. . .' (Eph. 4:22–3). Matthew tells us that the kingdom of heaven is taken by violence (Matt. 11:12). What we must remember is that the force for this violence does not come from mere human power, it comes from the new life within. Our battle is to get our wills in line with the One who lives within us. Our self-seeking wills need to be put to death, not by our power, but by the death of Christ.

REFLECTIONS

- What is important is to try to live, not by our feelings, not by our reasoning, but by the truth. There is a power within us. We do not learn to use this power overnight. Someone once said: 'Self-will dies half an hour after we do.'
- Try taking one truth and spending some time meditating upon it. See if you are able to let that truth affect the way you live your life today. In the evening see how you did. It took time to learn to ride a bicycle. Rome was not built in a day. Steady perseverance is necessary.

4

Sacraments

As well as having a living faith which constantly brings Jesus' saving power to us, there is another way in which we receive what Christ has done for us: this way is through the sacraments.

Although God has chosen to work through sacraments, he is not obliged to do so and he is not restricted to working through them. He is God and he can give his gifts to whomsoever he wishes and in whatever way he wishes. Sacraments are for our comfort. Whenever we see certain signs and hear certain words, provided there is no obstacle on our part, then we have the guarantee of the Church that what Jesus achieved all those centuries ago is now being made effective in us. This is of great comfort because it is not a matter of feeling that something is happening, nor of understanding how it happens – it is a matter of believing and receiving.

Baptism

To begin with, obviously, baptism was given to adults who had freely chosen to be united with Jesus, and had asked to be baptised into the body of believers. Faith was required of these candidates.

With the high rate of infant mortality, parents became anxious when their children died before being old enough to receive baptism, and this prompted the Church to grant permission for infants to be baptised. The act of faith was now required from the parents and godparents, whose duty it was to lead the child to make his or her personal act of faith and acceptance when a suitable age was reached.

I have great sympathy with the Baptists who insist on adult baptism, because when parents fail to lead their children to make their own act of acceptance, we can end up with baptised people who have never appropriated their baptism. The Catholic Church accepts infant baptism and holds that such a sacrament is valid, but if that sacrament is not fully accepted at a later date, then in some way the full effect of the baptism is blocked. We must remember that sacraments are not magic, they need to be accepted deliberately.

We are born sinners; we do not become sinners by sinning, rather we sin because we are sinners. On Calvary, Jesus, who had been born into wounded nature, laid down that nature in death. In doing this he paid abundantly for all human sins. When he rose he did not come back to life in his Adam nature, he rose to new life and became the new Adam, the initiator of a new family.

Jesus told us that in order to enter this family, we had to be born of water and the Holy Spirit. We, too, have to die as he did to the Adam life, and rise to new life. We do this in Christ. What Christ did two thousand years ago is made present and active to us through the Holy Spirit.

Sacraments make real what they portray. In baptism we go down into the water signifying going into the tomb with Christ, laying down our Adam life. Rising up out of the water we rise to new life in Christ. What happened at Calvary has now happened in us. All this takes place within our spirit, we do not sense this new life in any other way. It is only as we draw on it in faith that we will experience its power. Being born of the Spirit does not give us instant spiritual maturity, just as natural birth did not give us a fully developed, mature human nature. Very slowly and gradually we acquire human skills, and this is also true in the spiritual life.

As we will see later when we talk about being baptised in the Holy Spirit, the charismatic renewal has brought many baptised adults to appropriate their infant baptism. If someone is left a fortune but never told about it, then that fortune is of no profit. And so it is with baptism: many have come to understand who they are in Christ Jesus and thus have experienced a surge of new life within themselves.

Eucharist

As we have seen, on Calvary Jesus paid for our sins, and all Christians have continually to put their trust in what happened there. At the last supper when Jesus commanded his disciples to 'do this in memory of me' (Luke 22:19), I am sure they did not realise at first just what he was asking them to do. For when he took bread and said 'This is my body' and then took wine and said 'This is the cup of my blood', he was making it possible for his sacrifice on Calvary, where his body and blood were separated, to be made ever-present to his Church.

At Mass we do not repeat Calvary, that cannot be done, but we make it present to us through the sacrament, so that we may allow it to have deeper and deeper effect in us as we bow before the mystery made present.

God in his great mercy allows us the opportunity, time and time again, to say our 'yes' and 'thanks' to his Son who gave his life for us. This is wonderfully expressed in the words of some of the prayers said over the gifts, as the following examples illustrate. 'Father, may we celebrate the Eucharist with reverence and love, for when we proclaim the death of the Lord, you continue the work of his redemption' (second Sunday of the year, cycle A). The same idea is expressed in the nineteenth Sunday: 'God of power, Giver of the gifts we bring, accept the offering of your Church and make it the sacrament of our salvation', and again on the twenty-seventh Sunday: 'Father, receive these gifts which our Lord Jesus Christ has asked us to offer in his memory. May our obedient service bring us to the fulness of your redemption.'

Through faith and this sacrament, we are able to expose ourselves to the mighty salvation which took place on Calvary. Through our uniting ourselves to

Jesus by eating and drinking his body and blood we embrace and make ourselves one with the Lord who has stood in for us and paid our debt. Again what has happened in the past is made effective to us every time we celebrate the eucharist.

Reconciliation

Although Jesus empowered his disciples to forgive sins, we have no record of this sacrament until the third century. This does not mean it did not happen, only that we have no record of it.

The words of absolution, now thankfully said in English, give us a clear picture of what is taking place.

God, the Father of mercies, through the death and resurrection of his Son has reconciled the world to himself and sent the Holy Spirit among us for the forgiveness of sins; through the ministry of the Church may God give you pardon and peace, and I absolve you from your sins in the name of the Father, and of the Son, and of the Holy Spirit. Amen.

Again, a past event is now, through the work of the Holy Spirit, being applied to someone who has confessed sins. Of course it is perfectly possible and right to confess to God in the privacy of our hearts, but it is for our comfort and consolation to be able to hear the Church say with full authority, 'I absolve you from your sins.'

So, too, with the other sacraments, the saving work of the Lord is demonstrated either through healing or equipping the recipient with salvation. In confirmation the Spirit of God brings us to a deeper level of maturity as children in God, able to give and receive spiritual gifts. In marriage we need a share in the love of God in order to be faithful and loving; we need courage to face the problems of life together, the problems of family and the heartbreaks of life. When sickness strikes we need to allow the healing hand of the Lord to be laid on us through the sacrament of healing.

God in his mercy and love has arranged that we can live a life in which his Son's redeeming work is always available for us to apply to ourselves. Sacraments are received at certain moments in life, but faith is always available for us to use.

REFLECTIONS

- Many of us are familiar with sacraments. Try and note any new insights you may have received from realising that sacraments are making effective in us what was achieved long ago. For example, I used to think that if I made a good confession then God forgave me my sins at that moment. I now understand that at the moment of confession he applies the forgiveness already won for me.
- Can you see the Mass now as Calvary made present and not repeated?
- Jesus is still present to us in 'his' Church and through the sacraments we can approach him and allow him to lay his hands on us, healing us, forgiving us, strengthening us.

● In the next chapter we turn our attention to the gifts of the Spirit or charisms as they are often known.

5

Gifts of the Holy Spirit

 The object of the charismatic renewal is not to establish prayer groups, rather it is to restore to the ordinary life of the Church the charisms, the spiritual gifts, the power gifts of the Holy Spirit. A charismatic gift is in operation when the Holy Spirit empowers someone to act in a way above their normal capability in service to another.

The word 'charismatic' is understood by many as denoting a lively character or an enthusiastic form of behaviour. Any person or behaviour that is exuberant, demonstrative or emotional is labelled 'charismatic'. Hence, for many 'charismatic renewal' means learning to pray with enthusiasm, with bodily gestures such as hand-clapping or raising arms into the air. I can understand how people can get this impression, but the fact is it is a wrong understanding. Such demonstrable behaviour need not be there, but if it is, perhaps it is giving expression to a deep joy.

As I say, charisms are spiritual gifts given, not for

ourselves, but in service of others. They are different from natural gifts which we use and develop for others at will; for example a teacher teaches others, a doctor through skill heals, a lorry driver transports goods from one part of the country to another. Spiritual gifts cannot be used at will. They are given at a certain moment and they should be handed on to another for their spiritual help. These gifts can bring healings through the spirit, spiritual messages or insights, miracles, or spiritual encouragement.

Spiritual gifts were certainly active in the early Church. Scripture refers to them in different books and we meet them in the early history of the Church. I think there are several reasons to explain why these gifts became almost lost to the Church. One reason has to do with the level of faith of believers. The early Church naturally attracted very dedicated people because to be a Christian in those days meant that you certainly lost your job and most likely your life. Therefore the Church's members would be people of deep faith, and where there is deep faith God can act with power. When Christianity became the religion of the Roman Empire many joined the Church for convenience, and the level of faith would have dropped markedly.

A second reason has to do with the growth of the Church. As it grew and expanded there came a need for more organisation, more legislation, more guidelines for decision making. This way of operating is in contrast to the exercise of spiritual gifts, which of their nature are inspirational. These two things, though, are not meant to be in opposition to each other, but are intended rather to be in healthy tension. If the Church becomes purely institutional, then it loses its vision and becomes just an organisation. When the Church depends on inspirational guidance alone, it can easily be misled.

However, the gifts never entirely disappeared and they would often manifest themselves in the lives of saints. Unfortunately this made people think that these gifts belonged only to the specially holy. Of course, it could be pointed out that saints are only normal Christians, and the rest of us are sub-normal. It is only in this century, however, that there has been a real rediscovery of the gifts of the Spirit and a renewed awareness that they are gifts for all Christians, not just a chosen few.

All Christians are filled with the Holy Spirit at baptism and are indwelt by him to enable us to live lives of faith and love; we have a responsibility to nurture the Spirit within us and to live by his promptings. However, the gifts of the Spirit are different. They are given specifically for the service of others and belong to the Holy Spirit, that is why we call them his gifts, and he, as it were, lends them to us for a certain moment for us to use. A prophet cannot prophesy at will. These gifts do not belong to us, and therefore we cannot turn them on as and when we desire. This is why all spiritual gifts must be tested; it is important to know which spirit acted – the Holy Spirit, the human spirit, or an evil one.

When a sacrament is given, there is no need for us to ask which spirit has operated. We have the guarantee of the Church, provided all was valid and legitimate, that God has acted; but when a spiritual gift is being used, we have no guarantee that God is the source of the gift. That is why all gifts must be tested. We will look at how they may be tested later on, but for the moment it must be understood that these gifts are not to be taken as God-given until proved.

The gifts of the Spirit must also not be confused with the fruit of the Spirit. The fruit of the Spirit is a sign of holiness, the gifts are not necessarily so. If you have a fruit tree and it produces good fruit, then you know you have a good tree. But if you have a Christmas tree loaded with the most expensive gifts, then those gifts tell you nothing about the tree.

Usually when a spiritual gift is manifested, then the person from whom it comes is used beyond their normal capabilities. Sometimes the Holy Spirit can enhance a natural gift, using the person in a way that is beyond their normal power. For example, someone with a gift for playing the guitar may be so anointed that they play the instrument in such a way as to anoint everyone who hears it at that time; or a person who is good with words may be anointed so that what they say moves people's hearts strongly.

The gifts are certainly scriptural, and in Mark's Gospel Jesus himself refers to them as signs of the believer (Mark 16:17). Some scholars claim this passage was not written by Mark but by someone else, but nevertheless it is part of the canonically accepted Gospel. St Paul refers to the charisms in his letters to the Romans, Ephesians and particularly to the Christians at Corinth. He explains these gifts in chapters 12 and 14 of his first letter to the Corinthians.

In this letter he gives a list of nine gifts of the Spirit. He starts off by saying that he wants to clear up a misunderstanding with regard to these gifts – he could well be writing today as there are certainly many misunderstandings around. There are a number of people who simply do not know about these gifts. They never seem to have heard of them, or if they have they have dismissed them as something belonging to past history. There are others who know about these gifts but simply are frightened of them and, if they are in a position to oppose them, then they do. Then there are those who misunderstand them and misuse them; as someone once said: 'I wish those who have not been given these gifts, would stop using them.' And there are those who learn about them and are open to them, but are wise and prayerful people listening to the Lord.

The nine gifts listed by Paul in his letter to the Corinthians can be divided into three sets of three. There are three which could be classed as 'doing gifts': faith, miracles and healing; there are three that could be termed 'spoken gifts': tongues, interpretation and prophecy; and there are three which could be identified as 'knowing gifts': words of knowledge, words of wisdom and discernment.

In the rest of this book, I will examine each of the gifts, and I hope we can come to understand better their purpose and the need for them to be a part of the ongoing life of the Church.

REFLECTIONS

● When did you first hear about charismatic gifts?
● Have you ever experienced others using the gifts of the Holy Spirit? Have you ever been used yourself?
● Try not to judge the gifts by whether you like

45

them or agree with them, but rather judge them by seeing if God gave them to his Church.

- Read what the Second Vatican Council documents say about charisms (Chapter 12 on the Church). This is the official teaching of the Church on the subject, and no matter what any priest may say to the contrary, it is still the official teaching of the Church.

- Cardinal Suenens said that if you light a candle you will give light, but you will also attract mosquitoes. The renewal certainly has attracted some odd bods, but we need to remember that everyone is loved by God and precious in his eyes.

6

Gift of Faith

'. . . Another the gift of faith given by the same Spirit'.
(1 Corinthians 12:9)

The charismatic gift of faith must not be confused with the theological virtue of faith. The charismatic gift is a passing power by which God moves someone to act with certitude. This certitude does not come from human reasoning; it comes from the Holy Spirit and causes a person to act with confidence as when the centurian said to Jesus: 'Sir, I am not worthy to have you under my roof; just give the word and my servant will be cured' (Matthew 8:8). This charismatic gift of faith is what moves mountains and is given only at certain moments in our lives. The virtue of faith, on the other hand, is a power which Christians have all the time. It is a condition of mind, a readiness to believe the gospel.

Many of the Old Testament figures, who already believed in God, also believed God's promises given at particular moments during their lives. Noah, for example, built an ark trusting in the Lord's word that there would be a flood (Genesis 6:13ff). I am sure as he built it he came in for quite a bit of ridicule and mockery, but he carried on regardless. Abraham left his home and country on the word of the Lord to go to a land he did not know (Genesis 12:1, 2). God told Moses at the Sea of Reeds to stretch out his hand and part the waters so that the sons of Israel could pass through (Exodus 14:16). This was no easy command to obey even if Moses heard God's actual voice.

However, the Old Testament is shrouded in the mists of time and we are quite prepared to accept that things happened then that we would not countenance now. When Scripture says that the Lord told Moses, we tend to take that literally; but if someone today said to us that the Lord had told them to do this or that, we would be highly suspicious. One reason for this is that it is not our experience to hear God speak like that. Also, it sounds just too easy to have God directing us from heaven. And anyway, if a person does hear a voice, whose voice is it? I wonder if we have become so rationalistic that we have left God no room to move?

With things of the Spirit we need a very balanced attitude. It is so easy to become totally gullible and believe everything on the one hand or to become a hard-nosed cynic on the other. It is far easier to look after a graveyard than a school-yard. In the former nothing happens, in the latter there is life, tears and laughter. If the spiritual gifts are to find their place in a parish, they will cause problems; and that is why love must be pre-eminent.

I cannot say that this gift of faith has been very

prominent in my own life, though I do remember that when I was wrestling over my call to be a monk, I read a phrase in *The Imitation of Christ* which totally changed my view of my vocation. I had entered the monastery at the age of nineteen and had spent four miserable years there feeling I ought to be a monk. Finally I left and had five glorious years in the world, though I have to confess that I could not settle down to any job. After my mother died I made a retreat and the retreat-giver told me to read *The Imitation of Christ*. It was not my favourite book at that time but I decided that since he had told me to do it, I would do it. I picked up the book and the first phrase I read was: 'Why are you always seeking to rest, since you were born to labour?' I confess it is not a very exciting phrase, but from that moment on I knew I was called to be a monk, and I have never wavered since then. I know that as I read the phrase it was as though I heard the Lord speaking to me. I did not hear a voice, but I knew with utter certainty that God had spoken.

This all happened long before I encountered the charismatic renewal, and even today if I ever tell the story I can feel people distancing themselves from me. After all it sounds quite wacky.

The trouble is when someone has a strong sense that they are being called by God to do something and we need to discern whether or not this is so, we cannot rely on human prudence. Prudence is a very important virtue, but cowardice can often parade as prudence. Again if we are not endeavouring to live in the Spirit then we will find it very difficult to recognise when a spiritual gift is operating. To live in the Spirit is to live, not by our feelings, nor by our reason but by God's prompting. The problem is, what *is* God's prompting?

I have seen simple folk step out in faith to believe that God is asking something of them, only to have it proved that they were wrong. I knew a couple who had been told that a healing would take place. I certainly admired their tenacious hold on the promise while the sick person was visibly fading in front of our eyes. When the person died, the result was devastating. Yet I have seen others obey a word, and time has proved that they were correct as, for example, when a mother listening to a talk on healing, felt strongly she should ask the speaker to pray over her small son. She obeyed the prompting and the child was set free from his problem.

I can well understand why priests feel very vulnerable when they are asked to give opinions on spiritual manifestations. We feel quite inadequate, particularly in the light of the fact that we ourselves were given very poor training in this area save that we must be very, very cautious. It is no wonder that the Church is so long in making pronouncements with regard to extraordinary phenomena. It is so easy to be carried away on the one hand or be too cautious on the other. There is, in fact, the warning in Scripture of even the chosen being deceived (Matthew 24:24).

As with all spiritual gifts they must be tested. This is done by prayer, a certain amount of common sense, and endeavouring to judge what sort of person is manifesting the gift, but all the time aware that 'God's ways are not our ways'. He can ask for something that by human wisdom seems foolish (building an ark); he can use people we would not choose (Moses stuttered); he can bring about what to us seems impossible (he multiplied bread). This is where the charismatic gift of discernment is so helpful. (I will talk about this in a later chapter.) But when we do not have this gift among us we cannot force it to be there. In its place we have to use human wisdom, which is so limited.

All members of a group should be called upon to help in the process of discernment. If someone has spoken what seems like a word of faith then we need to ask if others in the group have a text from Scripture to support what was said, or another word or a prompting. How did people feel when the word was spoken? What was the gut reaction? What is important is that we be as simple as doves yet as wise as serpents.

I have to confess that I have not had too much experience with the charismatic gift of faith. I have heard about groups feeling certain they were called to do something that put them into debt, and the debt was finally met on the very last day before the deadline by an anonymous donor sending a cheque for the exact amount without knowing anything about the debt at all. But, as I say, discernment within the group is essential.

It is not always easy to draw a line between the gifts, nor to decide which gift is operating. Sometimes healers know beforehand that someone will be healed, in which case either the gift of knowledge or the gift of faith is operating. At other times they have a tingling in their hands; I do not know what gift, if any, is in operation then – the tingling happens but is not necessary. There are other times when they just lay their hands upon individuals and healings follow; we then know a gift of healing was there. The charismatic gift of faith is a call to act and not just a call to believe in a doctrine.

Teaching about all these gifts is very important and then people should be encouraged to step out in response to the slightest promptings. Absolute honesty is of utmost importance. Mistakes will be made, and correction must be given. These gifts will never be used perfectly, a lot of human nature will get mixed up in them. That is why Paul insisted that wherever these gifts operate love must be over all.

REFLECTIONS

- Have you ever been taught about this charismatic gift of faith?
- This charismatic gift must be distinguished from the virtue of faith. A Christian always has the virtue of faith; it is there to be drawn upon. For example, believing what God has accomplished through the death and resurrection of Jesus enables us to live in the power of the Risen Lord. A charismatic gift of faith is a passing gift enabling someone to act with certitude in a certain situation. Try and think of examples of faith as a virtue and faith as a charismatic gift.
- Have you ever had a strong sense that you ought to do something? Perhaps you could not give any clear reason why, except that you felt obliged to do it. Did you respond to that prompting? What happened?

Miircles

'... One may have the power of miracles'.
(1 Corinthians 12:10)

A miracle happens when God overrides or suspends the laws of nature. God is the cause of everything, and when he created this earth he gave certain natural laws so that there would be order in the universe. If and when it seems good for him to bypass those laws then, of course, being God he is free to do so. When Jesus multiplied the bread and the fishes, then the laws of nature were overridden.

There are times when it appears that the laws of nature have been suspended, but some trick may have been used to make it appear that way. A miracle is when it has been proved that there is no natural explanation for what has happened. This is why the Church is slow to accept miracles and careful and thorough investigation has first to be carried out. Coincidences are not miracles. If you have prayed for a parking spot outside the supermarket and as you drive in a car drives out, that is not a miracle for no law of nature has been suspended. If, however, the car drives out without a driver, then you have every reason to suspect that you are witnessing a miracle.

Jesus did many wonders and miracles in his lifetime for he was inaugurating the kingdom of his Father showing by his works of power who was master on earth. Adam and Eve had been given the earth and made responsible for its development. When they submitted to Satan, the earth became his. Jesus came to claim the earth back for the Father and he shows by his power that he is master of the earth.

While I was growing up I was taught that miracles and healings could still happen today, but I was also led to believe that they would be very rare and the chances of my ever seeing one of these marvels was extremely remote. If I am honest, my experience of religion was not one of liberation, for I was encouraged to embrace sufferings, carry the cross and be suspicious of anything I enjoyed. I do not think I was craving to do evil, I just seemed to want to enjoy life. Discovering that the Lord was actually on my side, made me see the gospel in a different way. There was a victorious side to it, a side that said the Lord had overcome and in him I was able also to overcome and the Church's task was to administer the fruits of his victory to the faithful.

It was easy to conclude from my experiences that the reason why we had not witnessed any signs and wonders was because we had simply never dreamt they were possible. In the early days of the charismatic renewal I remember plucking up the courage to step out in faith and pray for a healing, and while a few good things did happen, there were no major miracles. But elsewhere things were happening and even if you take into account that stories are bound to get embroidered with the telling, there was no doubt that something was stirring. They were heady times.

What I found frustrating was that I never saw any major demonstration of divine power myself. I heard about them, talked to those for whom something wonderful had happened, but I never seemed to be there when they took place. As time went by we had to face the problem that although great things were happening, these things did not always occur when we prayed for them. Clearly, although we had over the years neglected this tremendous power given to us by the Lord, this power was not something we could demand and so solve the problem of suffering and hardship.

It is important to see that there are two themes in the gospel. The first talks about surrendering, letting go, losing life, dying, offering the other cheek and denying oneself. It could be called the way of 'negativa'. The other is in sharp contrast for it talks about victory, triumph, healing, setting free, driving evil away and establishing the kingdom of God.

Both themes are in the gospel and to stress one against the other is to give an imbalance to the message. Any over-stress on the 'via negativa' will give a very distorted picture to the gospel. If the gospel of triumph is highlighted, then false expectations are raised and we can end up believing that all our problems and difficulties will be removed if only we can muster up enough faith to claim victories left, right and centre. To adopt such think-ing is to head for trouble.

Jesus experienced both these sides of the gospel. He certainly saw power and victory in the early days of his public life. He cast out many evil spirits, healed many sick and calmed the storm on the sea of Gali-lee. Yet, none of those triumphs actually conquered Satan, they only drove him out from where he was, leaving him free to fight elsewhere. What finally con-quered him was not some mighty, spectacular contest whereby victory came as a result of supreme power; it all came about as the result of powerlessness.

Here we face a mystery: God's plan was not to rout Satan by sheer force, rather he overcame him with what seemed like a surrender – a defeat. Jesus had the power to step off the cross, to blaze against the powers of hell with supreme power; but the Father's way was completely different, it was one of humble obedience. Adam and Eve, in a world where all was in harmony, had refused to obey God and had gone their own way. Now here was one of their own race submitting himself to the most difficult obedience in a world full of sorrow and disharmony. The holy One of God allowed himself to be stripped of everything, his clothes, his dignity, his friends, even his very life, and he stood in powerlessness in obedience to his Father. It was this submission to obedient weakness that undid the bid for indepen-dence enacted by our first parents and all their children. This man, who obeyed no matter what, was God and therefore his obedience was able to undo all the wilful acts of disobedience of his brothers and sisters.

So when Jesus said 'Follow me', he was asking us

to follow in the way he trod, a way of victory and also apparent failure. Salvation does not just mean getting to heaven; salvation is also about being freed from ourselves. If we knew nothing but victory and success, we would never manage any humility. It is in the apparent failures where the ego can die, where we let go of what is wounded and allow ourselves to be made new.

Gifts are what they say they are – gifts. We cannot cause them to happen, but we do need to be open to their happening. There is the famous miracle of El Paso in Mexico where a parish decided that they would hold a party for the people who picked over the rubbish dumps. To their embarrassment far more people turned up for the party than they expected, but the food never ran out. We are tempted to dismiss such stories as exaggerated, even fabricated, but this has been properly authenticated. There is a video all about it and it is called *Viva Christo Rey.*

So miracles can happen today and we need to be open enough to accept that truth, yet wise enough not to jump to conclusions that any extraordinary happening is an authentic miracle.

REFLECTIONS

- Catholics usually know about miracles. They have heard about Jesus' miracles and maybe they have heard of other miracles happening at various shrines. Have you ever witnessed a miracle, heard firsthand of a miracle, or experienced a miracle in your own life?
- Do you expect ever to witness a miracle?

- Are you open to such a thing?
- Do you feel that God would never do a miracle for you?
- Do you think miracles happen today?

8

Healing

'. . . Another again the gift of healing'.
(1 Corinthians 12:9)

 In one way the healing ministry is not new to the Catholic Church for most Catholics have been brought up to believe in the healing power of God. In the New Testament we read about the many miracles that Jesus did, and, from what the Church taught and from what we read in the lives of the saints, healing has continued down through the centuries. Most of us, I am sure, have never questioned any of this for one moment, but, on the other hand, we have never expected to meet anyone who has been healed, or to experience a healing ourselves and, as for being an instrument of healing, that has probably never crossed our minds. We have been led to think of healing as something very rare and special. We tend to believe that healing is for very holy people or that it only happens at shrines.

It was only when I became involved in the charismatic renewal that I began to realise that the gift of healing was being manifested today and that all Christians could pray for healing, not just a special few. From the Gospels we learn that the Jews viewed suffering and sickness as a punishment from God (and I think some Christians are tainted with the same idea): 'Rabbi, who sinned, this man or his parents, for him to have been born blind?' (John 9:2) Jesus' reply was that neither he nor his parents had sinned.

Jesus seemed to treat sickness as something not willed by God for he spent so much of his public life curing those 'suffering from diseases and painful complaints of one kind or other, the possessed, epileptics, the paralysed' (Matthew 4:24). Some sickness he blamed on Satan: 'This woman, a daughter of Abraham whom Satan has held bound these eighteen years – was it not right to untie her bonds on the sabbath day?' (Luke 13:16) But he did not blame all sickness on Satan; for example Jesus told the cripple at the pool of Bethzatha 'not to sin any more, or something worse may happen to you' (John 5:14). It is also worth noting that Jesus left many sick at that pool unhealed.

Jesus clearly intended his disciples to heal in his name for he sent them out in pairs with the instruction to preach the gospel and to heal the sick (Matthew 10:1; Luke 10:1). When he gave his final commissioning before ascending into heaven, healing is only mentioned as part of that commission in Mark's Gospel (16:16ff). In the Acts of the Apostles we see the apostles continuing the healing ministry. Therefore we can conclude that the Church, descended from the apostles, should continue this work of healing today.

There is enough evidence of healing in the early Church to know it was practised. After the apostolic times one can trace tendencies that saw healing as a support to the proclamation of the gospel – in other words the primary purpose of healing was seen to be to confirm the gospel teaching rather than to relieve sickness.

With the Gnostic and Manichean influences, which downgraded the body, there was a lessening of the healing ministry, and thinking in the Church moved towards the Old Testament idea of sickness as a punishment sent by God. Together with the influence of the Irish monks who stressed extreme asceticism, the whole idea of seeking relief from suffering all but faded.

The questions asked by the reformers as to the value of physical sufferings really got little further than questions. No alternative was offered. The Council of Trent redefined the sacrament of extreme unction to confine it to those in danger of death and thus it remained until modern times. However, in spite of these attitudes, throughout this period healings did take place during the lives of saints. These healings did not come as a result of the sacrament of extreme unction being administered, for many of these saints were not priests. It is as though God was all the time waiting for the Church to return to a normal and healthy view of suffering and healing.

In truth suffering and pain are a vast mystery. Some pain is a warning and it tells us that something is not right. It alerts us to a problem and in that way is a blessing. Suffering can also produce character. If we always have everything our own way we could end up spoilt. Often I wonder if pain only came after the Fall. If Adam stubbed his toe on a rock, would it not have caused him pain, or would he have been so perfect that he would never have stubbed his toe? It is an interesting question but I suspect a red herring here.

In order for healing to occur, clearly some faith is required. Jesus often asked the person seeking healing if they believed. Who of us has enough faith? It is equally wrong to try and work up a faith. Rather, the right attitude is 'Lord, I believe, help my unbelief'. But belief does not guarantee healing. I know of a sad case where a wife got cancer, and both she and the husband desperately stated they believed that the Lord would heal her. The cancer took its course and she died. No one could say they did not have hope that the Lord would heal. But what a devastation her death was for the husband.

I do believe that God can overcome suffering without removing it. He himself had to go through death and yet look what came out of his death. I believe the Lord is often saying, 'I will walk with you through this and we will make, what is negative, into something positive.' I have sometimes met with those who say that they are resigned to God's will, and I am not sure that is right. I believe there has to be some fight in us against the sickness even while we accept that we are sick. I have heard doctors say that when there is no fight in the patient for life, then there is very little that they can do. Much depends on how we are looking at life. If we look at things from an earthly point of view, we are bound to see problems, misfortunes, sickness as obstacles which need to be removed. If we are believers then no doubt we will ask God to do this. If he does not do what we want we may feel hurt, unloved and even bitter. 'If God loves me, then how can he not listen to my prayer?'

If, however, we look at life from God's point of view of eternity, then we will see all these difficulties in a different light. They will remain difficulties and we can certainly ask God to deal with them; but we will have a trust that God who has our eternal destiny at heart, will only allow troubles which can be used for eternal profit to touch our lives. He says to us at such moments: 'You and I can make use of these disadvantages, we can turn the tables on Satan who thinks he is going to upset you, for the very plan he uses to hurt you, we, together, can use for good purposes.'

It is not God who sends the problems; we live in a world where there are problems. He permits a difficult situation, even a tragedy, promising that a deeper good can come from it. This is all but impossible to see if we are looking at life from an earth-bound perspective, where everything is judged from our own point of view.

Sickness is not confined to the body alone, it can affect the psyche or the spirit. All these areas are closely related and what is a spiritual problem can manifest itself in the body. A simple example is that having to relate to a very difficult person, can cause a tightening up of muscles whenever that person approaches. This tightening of the muscles could begin to cause the body to react in some way.

We must also be aware of 'healing spirits' invoked by certain people who claim to have a healing gift. Evil spirits can affect apparent healings. We must only seek for healing in the name of Jesus. Also there is such a thing as a natural gift of healing. No spirit is invoked but in some way healing is transmitted from one body to another. There are machines which can make the aurora around the body visible and it has been noticed that after the laying on of hands the aurora is lessened. Something has been passed from one person to the other. This form of healing seems to be more natural than spiritual.

Those who feel that God has given them a healing gift will only find confirmation by using it and seeing if results follow. Love must be the moving power in us. We must be cautious not to act insensitively, nor to force people to have us pray over them. It can be helpful to have several people praying over the same person, for if a healing does take place, then no one is able to claim it was through them that the gift came. Also, when there are several people involved, then other gifts such as words of knowledge might well be given to help to direct the focus of the prayer.

Personal Experience

It might be helpful at this point to say something about my own first attempts at praying for healing. I have to say they were not very encouraging. A parent of one of the students in the school where I taught had been diagnosed as having cancer. Immediately the thought came into my mind, 'you must go and pray for healing'. I went hot and cold at the idea of it, and this wretched thought gave me untold trouble. I went from feeling guilty and cowardly, to wanting to rush in as maybe a miracle would follow. Finally I plucked up courage and I went to visit the sick person. At the end of the visit, just before I left, I asked if I could say a short prayer. Of course this was welcomed, priests are often expected to give a blessing. I do not think I could call the prayer that I made a bold prayer for healing, I simply did not have the courage. Eventually the person concerned died of the disease and I felt badly for a long time.

Early in the 1970s I returned to England from the USA and, because I had had some experience with the renewal, I was considered rather an expert and I was asked to address a gathering in Harrogate at the Holy Child Convent. What I spoke about was the power of the gospel for today, and obviously I referred to its healing power. I gave quite a good argument that the Church should be healing today, for I had done a lot of thinking and praying since those early days in St Louis. I knew that Scripture supported this view; I had heard of enough genuine cases to be convinced myself.

I must have given a good argument for at the end of the talk, to my horror, I saw a nun hobbling up to me and I knew what she wanted. I looked around to see who else would do the praying over her, but it seemed that they had seen her coming and had fled. What else could I do, but pray over her. I made a rather safe prayer, punctuating it with such phrases as 'if it be your will'. I told the sister that it did not appear to be God's will as she did not seem any better; and she, bless her, hobbled away from me.

You do not need much imagination to guess how I felt. I drove back home to Warrington alone that night and I had plenty to say to the Lord as I drove. I complained that he had been badgering me about this healing gift, and that day I had dared to preach on it, and even dared to lay my hands on someone and pray, but where was he? Was it his half-day? I have to say here that I feel it is right to be fairly familiar with God. That particular evening I felt badly let down and so was a bit flippant with him. I got no answer during the car journey.

About three weeks later I got a phone call from Harrogate, I cannot even remember what the call was about, but at the end of it the person said, 'Oh, that nun you prayed over was not cured, but she was so much better that she went back to teaching.' My reaction was: 'What will happen when I believe?' And that, I now see, is precisely the danger with these experiences. Having been very closed to the possibility of healing we now all move to the opposite extreme and expect it to happen every time we pray.

There is no doubt that some people do have a gift for healing. This does not mean that every time they pray someone gets healed, but it has to be noted that a good number do seem to get some blessing. I do believe that all prayer is answered, but it need not necessarily be answered in the way we would wish.

I remember hearing Kathryn Kuhlman, a powerful healer belonging to a Protestant Church, and certainly things happened at her meetings. May God forgive me but I was very suspicious all the way through her sessions. First of all I found it theatrical, I did not expect to see her on the stage dressed in an evening gown. The music was sentimental and I felt uncomfortable until she started to pray. I cannot really recall, now, what she said, but I know I sensed a presence came upon us. Then she started pointing

to a certain part of the theatre saying there was someone there with arthritis and would they come down
to be prayed for. Then she would point to another
part and again say what complaint that person had
and would they come down. You were not allowed
to go on to the stage unless she had invited you. I
had been hoping to be called up there but I had no
physical complaints.

After she had gathered quite a number of people
on the stage, she began praying over them. There
was a nun who said she had not been able to touch
her toes for a time, and there she was all but doing
acrobatics, she seemed so free. Some people she did
not have to pray over, for on their way to the stage
they received their healing.

In truth I now have no trouble in praying for
healing. I do not think I have a definite gift of healing, but certainly there have been times when God
did seem to do something. There is a lady in
Cornwall who swears that after I had prayed for her
she regained the ability to sleep. There was another
lady who complained of a migraine headache and
said it had gone after I had prayed, but there was
no proving this. But the one I have never forgotten
happened when I was giving a parish mission in
Bradford. The priest said to me one evening, 'Let's
go over and see Kath, a friend of mine, who has had
an accident on a sledge and damaged her spine'. We
went over and the poor lady was certainly in much
pain. We had coffee and then my friend and I prayed
over her and went off home.

Next morning while I was preaching Kath walked
into the church. My priest friend noticed she was
walking without a limp; I was so busy preaching I

did not spot it. Needless to say there was quite a commotion afterwards when the story got out. She had not felt anything during the time we prayed over her, but she slept that night for the first time since the accident. When she got up in the morning all pain was gone. Since then she has been back to the doctor and he says she should still be in great pain, for the back is not healed. It is now eight years since this happened and she is still fine. In fact she has gone on several hill-walking holidays.

Practicalities

People need to be encouraged to pray for the sick. Praying for the sick does not mean you are going to heal the sick; you are *praying* for the sick. You are asking God to heal. Perhaps later on you may become more bold as you pray and study the Lord's commands for he did tell us that what we bind or loose on earth is bound or loosed in heaven. I know Catholics apply this text to confession only, but there are many other texts where the Lord tells us that he has put power in our hands and we are to act in his name (Luke 10:19). To keep asking him to act when he has told us to act, can be a real failure to obey his commands.

Some people have had a tingling sensation or feel great heat in their hands – these can be signs that God is trying to stir us to act. We will only know by stepping out.

So to sum up: today there is a new move to under-stand the Lord's command to his Church to heal. There seem to be two ways healing can be given. There is the sacrament for the sick, once known as

Extreme Unction and reserved for the dying, now called the Sacrament of the Sick, and which is given for recovery. The other is the gift of healing which can come through any member of the Christian family.

When a gift has been lying dormant for many years it needs time before it finds its right place in the normal life of the Church. Mistakes have been made, people have thought healing can be obtained on demand. We still have to grapple with the question of healing and the mystery of suffering. There is still much to understand, and doctors, psychiatrists and priests can learn much from each other.

REFLECTIONS

● Do you believe in healing today?
● Have you ever asked for healing?
● Have you ever experienced either physical or psychological or spiritual healing?
● Does the idea of healing frighten you?
● Were you taught to embrace suffering and sickness because it was God's will? If so, how do you reconcile the fact that Jesus healed so many?

Tongues and Interpretation

'. . . Another the gift of tongues and another the ability
to interpret them'.

(1 Corinthians 12:10)

I never paid much attention to
the gift of tongues because I
never felt it could be of any rele-
vance to my life. The way I
understood Pentecost was like
this: the apostles, after receiving
the Spirit, rushed out excitedly
speaking their own language, as
I thought, and were heard
speaking the language of the
country from where the listeners came. Not being a
reader of Scripture I never, of course, came across
the text in 1 Corinthians where Paul says: 'Anybody
with the gift of tongues speaks to God, but not to
other people; because nobody understands him
when he talks in the spirit about mysterious things'
(14:2). At Pentecost, as I understand it now, two
miracles were happening: firstly the apostles were
talking in tongues, that is a language unknown to

anyone save God; secondly the bystanders heard them speaking in their own languages.

The rediscovery of this particular gift today has caused the greatest difficulty. When I first heard about tongues being used, I was suspicious but also curious. I had thought that 'speaking in tongues', whatever that meant, was what happened at the first Pentecost, but was not something people did today. What bothered me was the thought of being able to make noises as though I was speaking in a foreign language, because as a child I used to do this with my brothers. I never dreamt that I would be able to speak in tongues because I felt I would never be sure if it was me or the Holy Spirit speaking.

I came across the gift rather dramatically when I was living in the USA and was visiting a Benedictine monastery at Pecos in New Mexico. Through over-work, I think I had exhausted myself for I was feeling drained of energy and enthusiasm. At one of their prayer meetings I heard a monk praying in tongues, so I decided to do what I had learnt as a child. I said a prayer to God expressing that if he wanted me to do this, 'Well, here goes. . .' What was there to lose for I was among strangers and in a few days I would be over the hills and far away? Nothing dramatic happened – I felt rather foolish and went to bed believing there was nothing in it.

But the next day texts in Scripture and things said by the retreat-giver struck me very forcibly. It was as though I was being urged to ask myself if I really believed in the gospel. After what had been quite a long dark period for me, I seemed now to be getting some light. The question I asked myself was, 'Had this all happened because I had experimented with tongues last night?' I just do not know. Throughout that day I allowed myself to sing in tongues and I felt more and more at peace.

Not long after this I went to stay with a group of priests in Michigan who were trying to look honestly at this renewal. I was feeling fairly lost spiritually but was determined to throw myself into everything whole-heartedly. I was advised to use the gift of tongues in my own private prayer-time.

Three days later, just after I had finished doing this, I felt I suddenly understood the gospel for the first time. It was as though I heard God say: 'Why are you so afraid of me? Can't you see I have made you my son, why not live as my son?' It is strange that a truth I must have heard many, many times, suddenly burst on me as though I had heard it for the first time.

This did not mean that from then on all was plain sailing; no, I had now painfully to apply this truth to all my false attitudes, false assumptions, anxieties and fears. Slowly I began to see that the gospel was not about performance and doing one's best, but about receiving life, forgiveness and love.

It is important to remember that God deals with each of us as individuals and that my story is *my* story. I do not think everyone has to speak in tongues, though I believe it should be more common than it is; nor do I believe that everyone can learn to speak in tongues by being told to babble. It is a gift from God and for each one of us it will be different, and while some of us may need a kick-start to get us going, others will find it happens very easily.

So what is speaking in tongues all about? Basically, when people pray in tongues they allow the Holy

Spirit to pray in them using their voice to utter syllables which mean nothing to them or to anyone who might hear them, for they are directed to God. St Paul refers to this when he says: 'The Spirit too comes to help us in our weakness. For when we cannot choose words in order to pray properly, the Spirit himself expresses our plea in a way that could not be put into words. . .' (Romans 8:26).

In the description of Pentecost in the Acts of the Apostles, it is not too easy to see exactly what happened. It would seem that when the Holy Spirit came 'They were all filled with the Holy Spirit and began to speak foreign languages as the Spirit gave them the gift of speech' (Acts 2:4). Other translations say 'foreign tongues'. Does this mean the apostles spoke in a known language or did they speak in a heavenly language? It is not clear. I take this to mean that the apostles received the gift of tongues at that time. Presumably this all took place in the upper room. Then in verse 5 it goes on to talk about devout men living in Jerusalem who assembled because in some way they were attracted by the commotion. Whether these men went into the upper room, or the apostles burst out of it into the streets is not clear, but on hearing the apostles speaking they each heard them in their own tongue. So not only was the gift of tongues being manifested but also there was the miracle of everyone hearing in their own language.

Normally, however, this gift of tongues is not the ability to speak a known language that you have not learnt, though, as at Pentecost, there have been instances where someone has spoken out making noises that were unintelligible to them but which were actually a language known by someone else present. This is not really what speaking in tongues is about. Remember the text quoted earlier: 'Anybody with the gift of tongues speaks to God, but not to other people; because nobody understands him when he speaks in the spirit about mysterious things' (1 Corinthians 14:2).

This gift is mentioned a number of times in the Scriptures and Mark tells us that Jesus said it was a sign of a believer (Mark 16:17). The place where we meet it most frequently is in the Acts of the Apostles, where we see the new Church being established.

So clearly this gift was active in the early Church. St Augustine refers to it as 'singing in jubilation' in his treatise on Psalm 32 (sermon 1, 7–8). 'It means to realize that words are not enough to express what we are singing in our hearts.' I do not think that this means the gift is only used when we feel very joyful, for it can happen when we are unable to pray because of some heaviness, 'the Spirit comes to help us in our weakness' (Romans 8:26).

I think the very fact that we cannot get our reason wrapped round it, is why this gift causes so much trouble today, it makes us afraid. Whenever there is something that the human mind is not able to explain, we can become over-cautious and suspicious.

Strangely enough contemplation does not seem to have the same effect and yet that certainly is beyond the grasp of the mind. Maybe some think of contemplation as having heavenly thoughts, visions, or experiences of being taken up to the seventh heaven. In my understanding contemplation is when our mind, having thought every thought about God, decides that there is no thought that can catch

God, and so it gives up thinking and becomes more content with just knowing God is there. Not being able to find any adequate thought we are content with just loving him and being loved by him. One no longer tries to think thoughts but is content with a presence. I think in essence tongues is similar: in contemplation you cannot find suitable thoughts, in tongues you cannot find suitable words.

Our voice, of course, is very personal to us; it is unique. If anyone could use my voice they would, in a sense, possess me. They could say with my voice, 'I, Ian, say this to you'. To allow the Holy Spirit to use our voice is to surrender very deeply to him. When we pray in tongues we submit our mind, the thing we value most. Often it is the beginning of a new relationship with God, because it involves such a deep surrender. But the Holy Spirit does not force us, we have to allow it to happen.

Normally this is a private gift to be used alone, but it can and does happen that a group all feel moved at the same time to worship God in tongues. A group can sing in tongues and it is an extraordinary experience to hear a very large crowd all singing different tunes, with different sounds and yet the whole making an exceedingly beautiful harmony. I do not know of any instance in Scripture where it is reported that a group has sung in tongues. As I said earlier, St Augustine referred to singing in jubilation.

The first time I heard a group singing in tongues I was amazed at the beauty and harmony of the sound. Another strange thing was that it started quite unexpectedly and ceased just as suddenly as though some unseen conductor had given the sign. Others have found the experience quite unnerving.

In the early days of renewal when people questioned me on tongues, some asked if I would give a demonstration. I would always answer that while I could babble, I would not be sure that it was the Holy Spirit prompting me. All the gifts can be mimicked but we cannot turn genuine gifts on at will. Tongues can very easily be forced and groups need to be on their guard against feeling pressurised to use tongues when the Spirit is not prompting. I am sure most of these gifts come when we have our focus on God and not on what is going on around us. I think there has to be some prompting from within to which we respond, and as I have said, it is usually a gift to be used in private.

Tongues and their Interpretation

Not all tongues need interpreting. For clarity's sake let's call the tongue that occurs during a prayer-time 'praying in tongues' and the tongue that needs interpreting 'speaking in tongues' or 'a message in tongues'.

A message in tongues is when an individual speaks out alone, loud and clear, in tongues. Everyone then should become quiet and listen. When the message finishes, all should pray that an interpretation will be given to someone. This is not a translation for no known language has been used; an interpretation is when someone senses what God wants said at that moment.

Sometimes one of the group may have been getting a thought, a prophecy, and have been wondering whether to share it or not. Tongues, coming from another, can encourage that person to speak out.

I have been present in situations when someone spoke out in tongues and we all waited for the interpretation. I wondered why the Lord did not give a prophecy in our own language; why did he have to prompt one individual to speak in tongues, and another with an interpretation? The answer could be that in this way he is showing us the unity we have in sharing the same Holy Spirit.

I was once at a small meeting when someone spoke out loud in tongues. I remember feeling tense because there were so few of us; in a large crowd you can always hope that someone will speak up. As the tongue was being spoken I had a text from Scripture in my head, but I was very new to all this so I sat there not saying a word. After what seemed an awkward time, someone spoke out the very text that was in my head. Was that a coincidence or was it God? A sceptic will say 'coincidence', a simple soul will say 'it was God'. I think a wise person will ponder deeply.

I think we all need to ponder deeply about this gift. It is in Scripture (1 Cor. 14:27-8). It is called a gift of God and we need to be careful before we reject it. God does not do anything without good reasons. The Second Vatican Council affirmed that the charisms are not just for the early Church but are for the Church of today. God's ways are not our ways.

REFLECTIONS

- Have you ever given much thought to the gift of tongues? Most people associate it with what happened at Pentecost and never dream that the gift is available to any believer. Has that happened in your case?
- Does the idea of this gift frighten you? If so why?
- Have you ever heard anyone speak in tongues?
- Have you ever, when alone, sung in a made-up language?
- Do you think God might have been prompting you to launch out into something you cannot exactly explain so as to set you free from being strictly logical?

10

Prophecy

'... To another the gift of prophecy'.
(1 Corinthians 12:10)

Prophecy is not about foretelling the future. Prophecy is when God reveals his heart and mind, through a person, to an individual or to a group. The message may concern the future or it may not; it could be a warning or a correction about some past event or it could be a message of comfort in a time of trial.

God spoke to his chosen people through his prophets. Moses led them out into the desert telling them that God was leading them into the promised land. Nathan was used by God to rebuke David for his sin; Isaiah spoke many messages of comfort and consolation to the Jews in exile. Prophets did not belong only to the Old Testament times. In his letter to the Ephesians, for example, Paul lists prophets among those chosen by the Lord to serve his Church (4:11).

God speaks to each of us in many ways but we often do not recognise it is God speaking. Samuel, for instance, thought it was the high priest calling him when God first spoke to him. If we are closed to the idea that God can and does speak to us, it is not likely that we will ever be used as a prophet. On the other hand if we are one of those people who is not able to tell the difference between a good idea and a God idea, then, alas, we will imagine we are getting messages when we are not. It is not easy to explain how a person knows when God has spoken to them. This is why all gifts of the Spirit need testing to see from what spirit they come. St Paul says, 'Never try to suppress the Spirit or treat the gift of prophecy with contempt; think before you do anything – hold on to what is good and avoid every form of evil' (1 Thessalonians 5:19–20). St John repeats the warning: 'It is not every spirit, my dear people, that you can trust; test them, to see if they come from God; there are many false prophets, now, in the world' (1 John 4:1). We must know which spirit is at work, God's Spirit, a human spirit or an evil one.

Obviously anything said that contradicts Scripture cannot be of God. But just because it does not contradict Scripture is no guarantee that a prophecy comes from God. Today we are witnessing a plethora of visions and locutions telling us to repent, fast, and pray. All these are good things, but it is no guarantee that it is God who is actually sending the messages. The Church adopts a long slow process before she accepts such things; we have to be as wise as serpents and as simple as doves, which is no easy task! It is far easier to be a sceptic or a naive person.

Just as in ordinary human communication, where

there can be a problem of misunderstanding or of colouring what we have heard with our own ideas, so, too, this can happen with visionaries. The vision may be of heavenly substance, but the one who receives it is still human and can err, and the message they pass on may be greatly influenced by their whole cultural background. In prophecy the message may only be 20 per cent of God and 80 per cent of the prophet. Such happenings are not done deliberately by the person giving the message, and often it takes quite a time before they become a reliable prophet giving us God's mind.

The testing that I have been talking about is very much a human gift. We deliberately test the message given by reason, by checking with Scripture and by a lot of common sense. There is also a spiritual gift of discernment, and we will talk about that in a separate chapter.

The first time I heard a prophecy given was at a prayer meeting held at the Visitation Convent in St Louis, USA. Prayer meetings were something quite new to me and I did not feel very comfortable being there. I sat right at the back so that I could make a quick get-away if something untoward happened. I was sitting on the edge of my chair feeling very awkward when suddenly in one of the quiet periods a voice spoke out very clearly: 'Why are you so afraid? Can't you see I am present?' That word went right into my heart and I was certain it was spoken to me. The person who uttered it was a long way from me and clearly they had not spoken because they saw me looking awkward. I remember thinking and asking myself, 'Why am I so afraid? I am a Benedictine and my life is spent in praising God and that is all that is happening here. True the songs are somewhat different to what I am used to, but all the same, God is being praised.'

A message spoken out during a meeting may not be relevant to everyone, and because it may not speak directly to us we must not therefore imagine it is a non-prophecy. It may well be for someone else. That is why it is a good practice for a person touched by what is said, to speak out about what the word meant to them. In a prayer group setting it is an encouragement to the person who spoke the message, and it also helps the leaders to know that the message seemed genuine. In other words it is a way of testing the message. If, on the other hand, no one responds to the prophecy, and the person who gave it is one who speaks out a lot, then the leaders of the prayer meeting may have to talk to that person so that everything may be done in peace.

It is not easy helping people know if they are being prompted by God or just a good idea. I think we need to encourage people to speak out when they feel a prompting, as it is only by trial and error that we can learn. If during a meeting a person gets a phrase or an idea, then they should be encouraged to ignore it to start with. If it keeps recurring, or if a reading from Scripture shared by another seems to confirm it, or the same happens with another spontaneous prayer or prophecy, then it is best humbly to share the thought and see if it is helpful to another. Mistakes will be made, but in love we dare with each other and we grow. Pride is in all of us and we can often be driven by a hidden desire to be of importance. As we shall see in the chapter on prayer meetings it is love, not gifts, that make prayer meetings blessed.

Prophecy is not, however, confined to the prayer meeting. During a counselling session the counsellor may be given a word for the person counselled. It could also happen in a sermon, or even when two people share spiritual thoughts together during an ordinary conversation. I heard of a priest once who during his sermon lost the thread of his thought and for a few moments while he tried to remember his plan, he just spoke out a few ideas. Afterwards in the sacristy someone came and thanked him for his sermon. Being human he was interested to know what part had been so helpful – it was the bit where he lost his theme and just filled the gap with a few words.

Writers can be prophetic and can be used powerfully by God to convey God's thinking to us. A person need not know that they are being used prophetically while they speak. It is often very difficult to distinguish between a fine thought, obviously prompted by God, and a prophecy, when God uses another in a way far above their capability. Spiritual gifts can be mixed with natural gifts; a person with a fine voice, for example, can be so anointed during a song that they lead listeners to a profound worship of God.

As with all these gifts we need to be as wise as serpents and as simple as doves. We need each other to protect ourselves from imagining that we are God's gifts to the Church. Of course, we are God's gifts to each other but not because of what we do but rather because of who we are.

REFLECTIONS

● Do you ever, while in prayer or in study of Scripture, have a sudden clear sense of understanding God's plan or purpose? It could be God is giving you insight into his mind. Jesus did promise that the Holy Spirit would lead us into truth (John 16:13). If that insight concerns another person or a situation, then it could be a prophecy.

● Have you ever while praying for someone had a clarity of God's plan for them or a sense of their inner burden? This could be a word of knowledge or a word of wisdom. Prophecy is usually a word from God to the person.

WORDS OF WISDOM AND KNOWLEDGE

11

Words of Wisdom and Knowledge

'To one there is given through the Spirit the message of wisdom, to another the message of knowledge by means of the same Spirit'.

(1 Corinthians 12:8 NIV)

There are several ways of gaining knowledge. The first, the normal way, is through the use of reason. Spiritual truths, however, though not contrary to reason, are beyond it, and we need God to assist us to accept them. The Holy Spirit has to help us as we think about revealed truths. As we ponder and wrestle with them, the Holy Spirit gives us understanding that could not be reached by reason alone.

Human reason can grasp the facts of divine revelation, but we need the Spirit to give us that interior illumination that only he can give. For example, the mystery of the incarnation means that the second person of the Trinity became a human being. A person may be able to grasp the fact of the incarnation, but his reason may want to reject it because

99

it cannot see how God, who is everywhere, can now only be somewhere; or how he who is almighty, now has limited strength. It is the Holy Spirit who is able to make such truths, which seem contrary to reason, become acceptable and life-giving.

This spiritual knowledge given by the Holy Spirit is both for our own spiritual growth and also for others. At baptism the Holy Spirit gives us gifts for our own spiritual life. At confirmation he turns us towards others so that we may become full functioning parts of the body, both receiving life and giving life. The seven gifts of confirmation are both for our own growth and also for service to others. The kind of knowledge and wisdom referred to in these gifts is the knowledge and wisdom into which the Holy Spirit leads us, as we wrestle to understand divine revelation.

In Section 11 of the documents on the Church from the Second Vatican Council we read:

Incorporated into the Church through baptism, the faithful are consecrated by their baptismal character to the exercise of the cult of the Christian religion. Reborn as sons of God, they must confess before men the faith which they have received from God through the Church. Bound more intimately to the Church through the sacrament of confirmation, they are endowed by the Holy Spirit with special strength. Hence they are more strictly obliged to spread and defend the faith by word and by deed as true witnesses of Christ.

In addition to the above there are other kinds of knowledge and wisdom, given by the Holy Spirit, which differ from what I have just described. These concern the charismatic gifts of wisdom and knowledge. With these gifts it is as though knowledge comes directly into our mind which is not the fruit of our reasoning processes or of our wrestling with revelation, but is suddenly placed there. This process is not easy to explain since it does not occur by the ordinary means of one thought leading to another, but as a direct revelation from God. If what is known is a piece of wisdom which helps to solve a difficult problem, then it is known as a word of wisdom, or a message of wisdom, or an utterance expressing wisdom. If the message concerns a known fact about something or someone, then the message is called a word of knowledge, or a message, or an utterance expressing knowledge.

When Jesus healed a man who was both dumb and blind (Matt. 12) the Pharisees, among themselves, began to accuse Jesus of casting out devils by the power of Beelzebul. We read in verse 25 that Jesus addressed the issue, 'knowing what was in their minds. . .'. One wonders whether he just guessed, or whether it was obvious from the way they were behaving, or did he have a word of knowledge? Jesus also promised his disciples that when they were brought before rulers they would be given what to say (Matt. 10:19). Clearly God can and does put words of truth directly into our minds.

Words of knowledge or wisdom usually come during a time of prayer, especially when we are praying for individuals. The way they come varies; sometimes they come as a thought into our mind or as a picture, and they usually seem to come out of the blue. Sometimes just one word comes. For example, for no apparent reason, the word 'father' could come into someone's mind, or the word 'insecure' or 'deceived', when prayers are being said over an individual. It is wise not to act immediately, but rather to leave that word in the mind and see if anything else is said that might confirm it. If it keeps returning then it is best to share it.

Some people get pictures and they can be quite vivid. I had one once which really was quite strange, but because it made no sense to me I kept quiet about it. The picture I saw in my mind's eye was of a number of people standing in a room with lampshades on their heads. The lampshades were opaque and therefore the light did not shine through them but fell on the floor. Everyone stood there in a pool of light. As I have said, because it made no sense to me I did not mention it to anybody.

Quite sometime later I remembered the picture and had an insight into its meaning. With regards to the gifts of the Spirit I had felt a little left out. I never got pictures or words of knowledge or great insights into Scripture and I complained to the Lord about it. I now felt he was teaching me something through this odd picture of people with lampshades on their heads. He seemed to be saying that if those people with the shades on their heads would only step forward one pace then the light would go with them and they would see the next step. I felt God was saying to me, 'My word gives you enough light to take the next step'.

Quite soon after that, I was praying the office when a phrase from Psalm 119 leapt out at me. It says, 'My word is a lamp for your steps' – this made me understand that the Word of God was not just to delight my mind, but was to direct my steps. I suppose that was a word of wisdom for myself. This could easily seem a bit trite but because of this experience of mine I can now understand other people's stories.

The problem with spiritual gifts that concern the mind is that they can be imagined, even contrived. Imaginative people can think a stray idea is a message from God and then we can get into all sorts of problems and trouble. That is why all gifts *must* be tested. We have to ask: was that God speaking, or was it the human spirit?

As with the other gifts, the gifts of wisdom and discernment are tested by making sure they are not contrary to Scripture or the teachings of the Church; did they hit the spot? was the word spoken true, helpful, encouraging? Obviously immature people can play havoc here, and that is why we need mature and spiritual leaders to guide and oversee what happens. Being open to the spiritual world does not necessarily mean you are in touch with God. There are good spirits and evil spirits. Jesus told us that he was the door, the gate, and that we have to come in and out through him.

Leaders need to encourage their members to use gifts. Teaching is necessary, followed by the encouragement to step out and offer their insights, their thoughts or pictures. Gradually the true gifts will be discovered. In chapter 14 of Paul's first letter to the Corinthians he shows that love is of primary importance, but he also urges the value of spiritual gifts. Gifts without love can be very divisive. Let's face it, in all of us there is ambition, a desire to be wanted, of use, valued. Love must both encourage and correct.

Teaching will help people recognise how these gifts work, and they must then be encouraged to step out and share their pictures, words, phrases. However, if these are not saying anything to anyone, then, maybe, at that moment the gift has not been given. It is important to realise that we are trying to be one body and not just a group of individuals with gifts. When one has a gift the whole body rejoices.

REFLECTIONS

- Had you ever heard about these gifts before reading this chapter?
- Do these gifts appear very strange and foreign to you?
- Even though they are scriptural, do you feel that neither of these gifts could ever be yours?
- If so why?
- Some people desire to have these gifts, some are afraid of them. Which are you?
- Can you see the value of these gifts?
- Can you also see their danger if not tested?

12

Discernment

'... Another may have the gift of recognising spirits'.
(1 Corinthians 12:10)

We cannot always depend on charismatic gifts happening. They are a gift from God; we cannot make them occur. God has given us his Holy Spirit, his Church and an intelligence, and we have a responsibility to make use of these gifts; but God, when he decides, can intervene and make some charismatic gift operate to help us. We need to be open to this possibility.

I have stressed, in talking about some of the other gifts, the need for discerning what spirit is operating. This is done by testing the spirit and to do this we use human discernment, that simply means we use common sense, we check that Scripture has not been contradicted (remembering that the absence of contradiction does not guarantee genuineness), and we also find out if the message meant anything to anyone – was it a strong message or just nice? We need also to consider the person who gave the message – are they stable, reliable, or perhaps highly imaginative (remembering, however, that God spoke through Shimei to David as he was being cursed by him, and also through Balaam's donkey)?

On the other hand the charismatic gift of discernment is when someone recognises which spirit is at work without having to go through the normal process of human discernment. The person just knows. This does not mean that others present should not use human discernment. They should note the fact that someone has claimed to have the gift of discernment, and then weigh that gift.

There are examples in Scripture of this gift of discernment in operation. Peter, for instance, when he confessed that Jesus was the Christ, was commended by Jesus for allowing the Father, and not flesh and blood, to reveal that truth to him (Matthew 16:17). Again, Peter discerned which spirit was working in Ananias and his wife Sapphira in the Acts of the Apostles. The converts were bringing gifts to the new community, some of them selling their properties and giving the proceeds to the apostles to help them in their work. Ananias and his wife Sapphira had sold their property, but at the suggestion of Sapphira, they kept back part of the money and presented the rest to the apostles. Peter immediately recognised that a fraud was taking place and he spoke out, accusing them of keeping back part of their gift. Clearly he assessed the situation by a gift of insight given him directly by God (Acts 5).

In the Old Testament the Psalms are full of references to God probing our hearts, knowing our thoughts, showing that God has access to our minds. 'Before ever a word is on my tongue you know it, O Lord, through and through' (Psalm 139:4). In the book of Jeremiah we read, 'I, the Lord, search to the heart, I probe the loins' (17:10). Solomon begged God: 'Give your servant a heart to understand how to discern between good and evil' (1 Kings 3:9). Evidently the people of the Old Testament comprehended that God was God and that he knew their inmost thoughts and could give inspiration directly into their hearts.

We are all subject to ideas popping into our heads and it is not easy to know exactly from where they come. They can originate from some deep-seated drive, a desire to be recognised or from a highly imaginative mind. God has access to our minds for he is our God and in his love and care he can prompt us with his inspirations.

Evil spirits also can influence us by putting false ideas into our heads in the hope that we will be led astray. So any thought that suddenly comes into our mind must always be discerned – where did that come from?

God can communicate with us in all sorts of different ways. When we use reason to solve a problem, God can speak to us as we work things out. When we are given a spiritual gift to use it means that God contacts us directly – we then act or speak not because we have reasoned something out but because God has enlightened us directly. Clearly our actions then need careful checking, and even the gift of discernment needs thoughtful consideration before it is acted upon.

Discernment is a very important gift for the

Church, and God in his wisdom and love has given this so that the Church will be protected from the evil one; therefore we need to know all we can about this gift and pray that the Church will have discerners and will encourage them.

Obviously, if we do not spend a lot of time listening to what God has said in Scripture and the Church, then it is not likely that we are going to be able to discern his voice when he speaks through other channels. We need to pray for the gift, not necessarily for ourselves, but at least for the body where the gifts operate. We also need to make sure we know what God has already said to us in his Scriptures and in the teachings of the Church. The more we are acquainted with what God has already said, the more we will recognise him as he reveals himself today.

The spiritual gift can be for discerning our own promptings. Is this thought from God or is it just me imagining? For example, I was reading a book the other day in which the author wondered if he was spending too much time talking about God and not enough talking with him. It hit me like a bolt out of the blue. I did not need much discerning – God had spoken forcibly to me.

If, on the other hand, I suddenly get the idea that I ought to open a coffee shop and thus be able to evangelise all sorts of folk that drop in for refreshment, then that needs careful discernment. Was that really God, or was it a bright idea? I need to talk it over with another person and we need to weigh it carefully, using all sorts of human skills. Care must be taken that we are not closed to God. This is not an easy area to discern, and that is why it is always wise to seek another's advice.

We must remember we are not asked to judge the message by whether we like it or not, but rather by whether we sensed God in the manifestation or not. Spiritual gifts require spiritual people to handle them properly and to recognise them.

Honesty and love in any group are of utmost importance. We can be tempted to keep quiet when we feel differently from what others think or say. If while a prophecy is being given, we feel that it is definitely not from God, then we ought to say so even if someone else says the opposite. We can make the excuse to ourselves that we do not want to hurt anyone, or who am I to say such a thing? This is false thinking, for it is not love to let something happen about which we feel unhappy. Far better to risk hurt than allow error to go unchecked.

As with all the other gifts careful teaching is necessary and then people need to be encouraged to offer what they think might be from God. Mistakes will be made, but that is the way we learn with everything. If we never did anything until we were certain that we had it perfect, then very little would ever get done. God majors on forgiving.

People need sound teaching on the gifts, which is not too easy to come by in these days when there is so much suspicion towards them. Encouragement needs to be given for people to step out and share what is in their minds and allow others to give their opinion. In this way love will bind us together and we shall be glad to have others who will talk honestly to us, and allow us to talk honestly to them. None of this is easy, especially as we live in a society that has learnt to be polite and imagine that that is being kind.

REFLECTIONS

- Can you see the difference between the virtue of discernment and the charismatic gift?
- Are you ever aware of your own spirit?
- How would you check an inspiration that came to you either at a prayer-time or outside it?
- Spiritual gifts usually require a certain spiritual maturity in the person in whom they operate. Of course, God can use anyone with his inspirations. Do you expect God ever to use you for discernment?

13

Baptism in the Holy Spirit

One of the things that worried me most, when I met the Pentecostal Movement, was the baptism in the Holy Spirit. What happened seemed very simple: a group gathered round a person and prayed that Jesus would baptise them with his Spirit. The effect was nearly always visible, either there and then, with the person becoming charged with a deep joy and happiness, or it happened quite soon afterwards. This had me puzzling: why didn't the sacrament of baptism have the same effect?

One could argue that most baptisms involve infants, but I have seen enough adult baptisms to know that there is usually no visible effect for those baptised. Theologically I could not answer the question, nor could I find anyone who gave me a satisfactory explanation. Many warned me that anything 'Pentecostal' was bound to have a lot of emotional exuberance.

While I could not understand what was going on

in this baptism in the Spirit, I certainly could tell from the results that something powerful was happening. God obviously became real for these people; somehow they knew Jesus and not just knew about him, he was real to them; they had an ability to praise God and do it out loud; they could witness boldly before others without embarrassment; they developed a great love for Scripture and would read and refer to it frequently; and often one of the spiritual gifts became active, most commonly, tongues.

I confess I never dared pluck up courage to ask for this baptism in the early days, though I longed for what it seemed to offer. As a priest I felt responsible, and I did not want to lead people into something about which I was not at all certain so I kept myself detached.

Now, some twenty-eight years afterwards, I think I understand what was happening. In the early Church baptism was given to willing adults. They had heard the good news about what Jesus had done for them, and they came willingly to receive all he had won for them – forgiveness for their sins and a new life in him. They came to their baptism with a lively faith, responding to God and his gift.

Today the scene is very different. Usually the one receiving baptism is an infant, so personal faith is absent, though there is faith, hopefully, in the parents and godparents. But even when the person is an adult there can, instead of faith in what Jesus has done, be more of a desire to belong to a Christian family.

Also the spiritual environment today is greatly different from earlier days when, even though infant baptism was practised, the child grew up in an atmosphere of faith. Living in a community of believers greatly strengthens the faith of all, leading the child to understand much better his or her own baptism.

Sacraments are not magic, they need to be given and accepted. Baptism and confirmation confer a supernatural gift, but ignorance or lack of understanding of the gift, can block its full effect. In other words, while the sacrament is valid and has been given, the effect has been blocked. When the block is removed then the full effect floods in.

I believe, through this renewal, many, many people have understood for the first time about the lordship of Jesus Christ and what he has achieved for them at such terrible cost, and they have seen clearly that Christianity is not about doing and then receiving, but rather receiving then doing. Therefore what has come to be called baptism in the Holy Spirit has been an opportunity for awakening in them their sacraments of initiation.

There is vast ignorance among the faithful today. Many have received a very sketchy understanding of their religion. Many have been educated after the Second Vatican Council, when it has not been at all clear what should be taught. While ecumenism is of such great importance, it is not easy to change a dyed-in-the-wool attitude overnight. And now that we are trying to build bridges with those of other faiths, there is considerable confusion among Catholics and Catholic teachers. We need very clear gospel teaching, and I believe the charismatic renewal has been one of the most important stirrings in the Church this century because it has evangelised the baptised.

There is no hard and fast way of receiving baptism in the Holy Spirit. All that is necessary is a real desire to receive what Jesus has achieved for us, but of course, in order to have that desire we need to know what he has achieved for us. The renewal has produced a seminar known as 'Life in the Spirit'.* This provides an ideal opportunity for people to go over the basics of the faith, which many have never done since their school-days.

We can ask another person, or a group, to pray with us for the baptism, or we can simply ask God for it by ourselves. Each year the Church offers us an opportunity to renew our sacramental baptism during the vigil service on Holy Saturday night; and that is what baptism in the Spirit is about. Do not judge the result of the prayer by how you feel. We must learn to live by faith and not by feelings. Feelings are not wrong; they are like the English weather – unreliable.

Jesus told us to ask and we would receive and he also said: 'If you then, who are evil, know how to give your children what is good, how much more will the heavenly Father give the Holy Spirit to those who ask him' (Luke 11:13). Again we have to hang on to the truth that Christianity is about receiving, then doing. We ask because we have need, not because we are worthy.

Because we are constantly learning more and more about God and all he has done for us, it is a good

---

* Further information about the 'Life in the Spirit' seminar can be obtained from the National Service Committee for Catholic Charismatic Renewal, Allen Hall, 28 Beaufort Street, London SW3 5AA.

practice to accept again and again, quite deliberately, our baptism.

REFLECTIONS

- Have you ever heard the term 'baptised in the Holy Spirit'?
- Have you experienced it, or have you ever suddenly had a second conversion or a clear insight into how much God loves you? It does not really matter what name you give to this experience, it usually means that the initiation sacraments are flowering in you.
- Do you understand that a 'born again' experience does not mean that is the moment you became a Christian, but means that is the moment when you realised the significance of being a Christian?

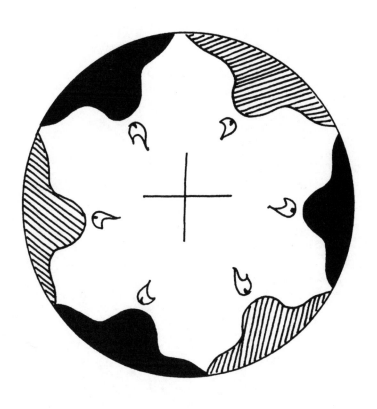

14

Prayer Meetings

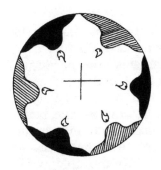 Many people think that the charismatic renewal is all about prayer meetings. But I must emphasise that the prayer meeting is not the essence of the renewal. The renewal is for the whole Church; prayer meetings are not for everyone.

Prayer meetings grew out of renewal. People had caught a new vision of God, and they wanted to praise and bless him, singing songs and canticles. Others who had not experienced this new vision of God, were attracted to these groups and had a new experience of prayer, often far deeper than anything they had experienced in a church service. Naturally they wanted to bring this experience home to their friends, their parish, and so they tried to set up a prayer meeting; but alas, often the initial new vision of God was not there, and it is very hard to praise God if he is not very exciting to you. Where a group of people had caught the new vision, then others coming to their meeting often were taught about this good God, and so they entered into the joy. Prayer meetings became very popular, and they spread like wildfire, but the mistake that was made was prayer meetings were being spread, whereas the good news about the Lord should have been spread. The result has been that many prayer meetings have become quite heavy, and although spontaneous prayer is there, the inspiration is often lacking.

Requires Discipline

A prayer meeting is much more than learning to pray out loud and being able to make up your own prayer. Obviously these elements are necessary, otherwise the prayer will not be shared; but there is far more to a prayer meeting than its spontaneity. A prayer meeting has to learn to pray as one body. That is really difficult to do. Take our human body: it is made up of many different parts, but it has to work in harmony to be a whole. For example, while I am typing this chapter, my legs do not exercise their gift of walking. Too often prayer meetings have become everyone praying out loud what they wish and when they wish. The result has been pretty chaotic. At first individuals may have felt a certain satisfaction in being able to pray out loud and contribute to the meeting; but if no one is really listening nor responding, then it is hardly one body at prayer. It is just a group of individuals praying out loud. Many prayer meetings started this way, but after a time the novelty wore off and they disbanded. Others have grown and developed as a body at prayer.

Let us look at how the Church prays. She gives us some thoughts about God's love for us or about what the Son has done for us, so that we may respond with thanksgiving and praise. In a prayer meeting it is the same; someone shares an insight or better still a Scripture passage, and then the group begins to respond freely to what has been shared. It may inspire someone to read another passage from Scripture related to what has been said; or it may inspire someone to thank God with a spontaneous prayer; another may want to sing a song that relates to what has been said; yet another may say a formal prayer that echoes the thought being shared. This is true spontaneity; it responds to the initial thought or reading shared. This requires discipline; we have to lay down our own ideas if they do not belong to what is happening at that moment. This also checks those who tend to dominate the meeting with their own ideas and thoughts. If the group is not well founded in the gospel and rooted in Jesus Christ, in other words if its members are not soaking themselves in Scripture between the meetings, then there is a risk that the sharing and prayers will be man-centred and not God-centred. Piety can flourish where solid gospel teaching is lacking. As I have said, many Christians need teaching in the foundational truths, and therefore prayer groups do need periods of teaching. Alas, there are not too many people equipped to do that but in time that will be remedied.

Simple a,b,c Rule

A prayer meeting does need a leader, not that he or she has to dominate or run the meeting. Someone is needed to start it off and bring it to an end. Also it is good to have someone who can prompt it when it gets lost or uninspired. A good way to start a prayer meeting is to get everyone to turn away from their concerns and worries by blessing and praising God for what he has done for us through his Son Jesus Christ. This period of praise is important. It can truly be a sacrifice of praise especially when we do not feel like praising. This time of praise should involve everyone. If the group has a good musician, then that is a great blessing because songs of praise involve everyone. There should be opportunities after a song for individuals to praise spontaneously or for the whole group to praise out loud together. Tongues can be used at this point. It takes time for a group to learn how to praise God. It is not done by trying to stir people's emotions, far better to get people to soak their minds in the great events that have brought us new life in Jesus. When the Spirit of God begins to make these events real to us, we will find praise welling up in our hearts. When we praise God we are doing the highest thing a person can do.

Some prayer meetings spend most of the time praising God and only towards the end is there an opportunity for someone to share God's Word through a reading or a prophecy. Other prayer meetings spend ten, fifteen or twenty minutes in praise, then sit to allow sharing of Scripture to happen. This is the time when the body tries to pray as one unit. When someone shares Scripture, then all reflect on what was shared and respond to it in different ways. In this way themes develop, different people give different insights, and the group grows because of each other's openness to God. This forms community, gratitude develops for each other, but our woundedness and selfishness are also brought up. There will be times when we have to confess to each other and ask forgiveness; there will also be times when we may have to confront one member with some fault. This is a time for real growth, and we move from just enjoying being with the group to become a loving community.

Towards the end of the meeting, the leader should, if possible, recap the meeting, pointing out what God seemed to be saying to the group, and then open the prayertime for special requests. This should be reasonably short. I have been at meetings where we have droned on, praying for every conceivable need, all very wearisome and counter-productive. All petitions should be made with hope in the risen living Lord. Finally a simple a,b,c rule can be helpful: a – be audible, b – be brief, c – be Christ-centred.

I have found that liturgical prayer, personal prayer and shared prayer, all nourish each other. Liturgical prayer taught me what personal prayer was about; personal prayer has taught me what shared prayer was about. But prayer without the renewal of one's personal relationship with God can become a blind alley. Prayer is very important, but it must not become an idol. Prayer must not become an end in itself, it must lead me to God, not experiences of God, but to God himself. That leads us to the final question: who is the God we pray to? What is he like? If we are wrong about him, then we will be wrong about everything that has to do with him, even our prayer.

REFLECTIONS

- Do you belong to a prayer group?
- Does spontaneous prayer threaten you? If so why?
- Do you like or dislike prayer meetings? Give reasons for your answer. Remember there are 'many rooms' in the Father's house (John 14:2).
- Do you prefer praying alone? Is that because you can escape the inconvenience of other people? This does not mean private prayer is wrong, it only asks are our motives wrong?

Epilogue

Taking authority, commanding in the Lord's name, acting in the power of the Risen Lord is certainly part of the gospel but it is also very seductive. Power, even if it is the Lord's, can appeal to our rebellious self.

If we have understood Christianity from a rather negative point of view, submitting and letting God have his way, it is very intoxicating to discover that we are sent out, in the power of his Spirit, to continue the work Christ came to do. It is no wonder my priesthood had seemed so powerless for it had never occurred to me to call on the power of the Lord, though of course I knew his power was in the sacraments, but my work involved much more than administering sacraments.

But is this power to be had for the asking? Peter was once delivered from prison, but there was a later time when he was led out and executed. I am sure many prayers were said for his deliverance on both occasions. I am also sure that many prayers went up from concentration camps, and yet the Lord did not intervene. Recently Bosnia and Rwanda have had all the eyes of the world focused on them, and I know many prayers have been said, but there has been no sudden miracle.

We must remember that God's ways are not ours. Today God has made his gifts of power appear again, but they are not for our glory, nor for us to use as we will. Pope Paul VI said of the renewal that 'It was a chance for the Church' and the present Pope has said:

The emergence of the Renewal following the Second Vatican Council was a particular gift of the Holy Spirit to the Church. It was a sign of a desire on the part of many Catholics to live more fully their Baptismal dignity and vocation as adopted sons and daughters of the Father, to know the redeeming power of Christ our Saviour in a more intense experience of individual and group prayer, and to follow the teachings of the Scriptures by reading them in the light of the same Spirit who inspired their writing. Certainly one of the most important results of this spiritual reawakening has been the increased thirst for holiness which is seen in the lives of individuals and in the whole Church.